The Basic Ideas of Calvinism

John Calvin
(1509–1564)

The Basic Ideas of Calvinism

Sixth Edition

H. Henry Meeter

Revised by

Paul A. Marshall

Baker Books
A Division of Baker Book House Co
Grand Rapids, Michigan 49516

CRC PUBLICATIONS

Sponsored by
Basic Historic Calvinism Committee
and
The H. Henry Meeter Center for Calvin Studies

First edition 1939
Sixth edition 1990
Second printing, May 1997
Copublished by Baker Book House Company, Grand Rapids, MI, and
CRC Publications, Grand Rapids, MI

Portrait of Calvin courtesy of the H. Henry Meeter Center for Calvin Studies, Grand Rapids, Michigan.

Library of Congress Cataloging-in-Publication Data

Meeter, H. Henry, 1886–1963.
The Basic Ideas of Calvinism / H. Henry Meeter.—6th ed. / revised by Paul A. Marshall.
p. cm.
Includes bibliographical references.
ISBN 0-8010-6269-1
1. Calvinism. I. Marshall, Paul A., 1948– . II. Title.
BX9422.2.M44 1990
230′.42—dc20 90-33204
CIP

For information about academic books, resources for Christian leaders, and all new releases from Baker Book House, visit our web site:
http://www.bakerbooks.com

Contents

Publisher's Preface

"There appears to be in many circles a renewed interest in the teachings of the great Genevan Reformer," wrote Louis Berkhof in the foreword to the second edition of *The Basic Ideas of Calvinism*. "This is an encouraging sign, for it would seem that these are needed today even more than they were in the days of the Reformation."

Interest in the teachings of John Calvin has not diminished since Berkhof wrote these words in the 1940s. Nor has the need for Calvin's theology. For this reason the Basic Historic Calvinism Committee deserves the gratitude of all for its efforts to see *The Basic Ideas of Calvinism* revised and republished once again.

The author, H. Henry Meeter (1886–1963), taught for thirty years in the Bible department of Calvin College. He had graduated from the same college and from Calvin Theological Seminary before obtaining a B.D. degree from Princeton Theological Seminary. While at Princeton he was offered two fellowships for scholarly achievement, one by B. B. Warfield in systematic theology and the other by William Park Armstrong and J. Gresham Machen in New Testament theology. Meeter accepted the former and pursued his studies further at the Free University of Amsterdam. He graduated in 1916, receiving a Th.D. degree cum laude. His dissertation, "The Heavenly High Priesthood of Christ: An Exegetico-Dogmatic Study," was published soon afterward in both the Netherlands and North America.

In 1926 Meeter accepted the chair of Bible at Calvin. Here he prepared several syllabi for his courses and two books: *The Fundamental Principle of Calvinism* (1930) and *Calvinism: An Interpretation of Its Basic Ideas* (1939). The latter went through three editions before its title was changed to *The Basic Ideas of Calvinism* (1956). The fifth edition, published in 1960, remained in print for almost twenty years. The first two editions were identified as volume 1, *The Theological and Political Ideas.* (Meeter was unable to complete two sequel volumes on other aspects of Calvinism.)

"A Christian gentleman and teacher of the first water: that was my initial impression of Dr. Meeter when I was first privileged to enroll at Calvin College," wrote his former student, good friend, and colleague John Bratt after Meeter's retirement. "Here, so it seemed to me, was a devoted and fully committed man of God, conscientious and industrious, one who threw himself heart and soul into the work to which he had been called and yet one who did not so engross himself in his work that he neglected the personal contact and the encouraging word."

"These first impressions were deepened by later course work under his tutelage," Bratt continued, "and when I became his colleague they were reconfirmed. He was always pleasant and cordial as of yore. The lustre of his kindliness and geniality had remained undimmed in the passing of the years. It was a pleasure and an honor to become his colleague. Then it was that I began to appreciate the weight of the teaching load he had borne singlehandedly throughout the years. God entrusted him with a rugged constitution and he did not spare himself. He gave himself unstintedly to his task."

"The author has for a number of years taught a course in Calvinism at Calvin College," Meeter wrote in the first edition of his book on Calvinism's basic ideas. "The purpose in this course was to present to the classes the salient points of the system. During the past few years, at the request of the Calvinistic Young Men's and Young Women's Federations of America he has been writing a series of articles for their monthly magazine *The Young Calvinist,* in which the aim was to state the basic ideas of Calvinism in systematic order and in semi-popular style. . . . The articles which have appeared in *The Young Calvinist* are herewith presented in book form to the reader. It is hoped that not only Calvinistic youth, but ministers, teachers, and intelligent laymen will find it a helpful guide to a systematic study of Calvinism."

The foreword to the second edition was written by Meeter's colleague at Calvin Theological Seminary, Louis Berkhof. "We know of no other work in the English language," wrote Berkhof, "which offers us such a concise, and yet complete and thoroughly reliable resumé of the teachings of Calvinism." Meeter's fellow professors at Calvin were not alone in their high esteem of his book. H. H. Kuyper of the Free University of Amsterdam wrote: "The purpose of his labor is especially to show the younger generation Calvinism in its multilateral meaning and Scriptural soundness, and through this arouse in them the love for Calvinism. And in this he has masterfully succeeded! That which was scattered here and there has been put together in a short and remarkable form and to a perfect and balanced unit."

Nor was the book praised solely by the Dutch Reformed community. The *Sunday School Times* printed a review calling it "a timely and much needed book." "It is probably one of the most valuable books on the subject since Dr. Abraham Kuyper's lectures on Calvinism were given in 1898," said the reviewer. Meeter's "interpretation of the theology of Calvin is sane and true."

F. E. Mayer, an American Lutheran, wrote in the *Concordia Theological Monthly*: "The book, very interestingly written, clearly shows that Calvinism is still a potent factor in the theological thinking of the modern Protestant. . . . We heartily recommend the entire volume as a very enlightening interpretation of Calvinism."

And the *Evangelical Quarterly* in London considered the book to be "sane and well balanced," giving "a bird's-eye view of Calvinism as a world-wide force" and showing "how its principles can affect profoundly all the relationships of men, whether religious, political, cultural, or international."

The Basic Ideas of Calvinism went through five editions and was translated into Dutch, Japanese, Korean, and Spanish. Now, after the book has been out of print for eleven years, Baker Book House could not be more pleased to publish this sixth edition.

Chapters 22, 24, and 25 are the work of Paul Marshall,

selected for this task by the Basic Historic Calvinism Committee. Marshall, who also contributed the reviser's preface, is senior member in political theory of the Institute for Christian Studies in Toronto. He holds a Ph.D. degree in political science from York University. (His chapters were reviewed and approved by the executive committee of the H. Henry Meeter Center for Calvin Studies.)

A new bibliography has been contributed by Peter De Klerk, theological librarian emeritus of Calvin College. De Klerk compiles the authoritative biliographies on Calvin which appear annually in the *Calvin Theological Journal* and is curator of the H. Henry Meeter Center for Calvin Studies.

An index has also been added to this new edition.

The text of Meeter's chapters has been only lightly copyedited by the publisher's editorial staff, who have largely confined themselves to relatively minor details of punctuation and form. Every effort has been made to preserve Meeter's distinctive style and usage.

May this new edition of *The Basic Ideas of Calvinism* extend the life of this important volume well into the twenty-first century.

Reviser's Preface

Making additions to someone else's book is an unusual exercise and one that presents certain novel problems. Any book whose last edition (1960) was several decades ago could be revised in a variety of ways—but then it would lose the imprint of its original author. On the other hand, if revisions were made in certain areas but not in others, then it might wrongfully be assumed that the editors believe that the unrevised items could not be further improved.

In order to limit both of these problems I have left Meeter's text largely untouched but have added three chapters (22, 24, 25). Two deal with issues that have grown in importance since Meeter wrote. One of these (chap. 22) deals with new questions about Christian responsibility in war which have arisen with the spread of means of mass destruction such as nuclear and biological weapons. The other (chap. 24) addresses the rise of and our proper response to "political" or "liberation" theology.

The third additional chapter (chap. 25) does not deal with a new issue but with a very old and recurrent one—the expectations we may have that our work will bear fruit. Because Meeter intended to follow this volume with a sequel (an intention which became impossible to fulfil), this book ended somewhat abruptly after a discussion of the Christian citizen and war. I believe it may be better to end on the note of some broader themes of Calvinism and, in particular, with the great hope that we have in Jesus Christ.

In writing these additions I have not tried to copy Meeter's style. However, I have tried to adjust my style to his in order that the transition between chapters is not jarring. I hope the result is not too unsatisfactory.

There are still several items in the text which remain a little awkward. Meeter's formulation "the Calvinist" sounds ponderous to the modern ear; his expression "the Roman Church" now has negative overtones; and the use of the masculine pronouns is now contentious. Furthermore, some of his views, such as that on "spirit" and "matter" in chapter 5, might be thought dualistic by contemporary Calvinists and I do not agree with his views in chapter 10 about what the state would be like had there been no fall.

Despite these cautions it must be emphasized that Meeter's work has stood the test of time well. His writing is confident, precise, and carefully organized. Perhaps its principal virtue is its clarity. He deals with difficult issues in a simple and forthright way, never going beyond the capacities of the general reader, but also never condescending to the reader. There is no other treatment of Calvinist theology and political principles that is at once so clear, so systematic, and so broad. It deserves our full attention.

In closing I would like to express my thanks to the Basic Historic Calvinism Committee at the H. H. Meeter Center for Calvin Studies for the opportunity to do this work.

Paul Marshall

PART

1

Theological Ideas of Calvinism

1

The Fundamental Principle

The significance of John Calvin for the modern era is vividly described in these words: "The sixteenth was a great century. It was the century of Raphael and Michelangelo, of Spenser and Shakespeare, of Erasmus and Rabelais, of Copernicus and Galileo, of Luther and Calvin. Of all the figures that gave greatness to this century, none left a more lasting heritage than Calvin."[1] To the investigation of the heritage of Calvin, the following pages are devoted.

Calvinism Is a System of Thought

Calvinism is the name applied to the system of thought which has come down to us from John Calvin. He is recognized as the chief exponent of this system, although he is not the originator of the ideas set forth in it. The theological views of Calvin, together with those of the other great leaders of the Protestant Reformation, are known to be a revival of Augustinianism, which in its turn was only a revival of the teachings of Saint Paul centuries previous. But it was Calvin who, for modern times, first gave the presentation of these views in systematic form and with the specific application which since his day has become known to us as Calvinism.

These teachings constitute a unity. Calvinism is not the mere aggregate of opinions, the sum total of ideas, held by Calvin and Calvinists, but it is an organic whole with one fundamental principle as the common root. It is not always or necessarily the case that the views of a group constitute a unity. The views of the Roman Catholic Church prior to the time of their great organizer, Thomas Aquinas (1227–1274), or officially prior to the Council of Trent (1545–1563), did not form a unity but lay scattered among the declarations of church councils and papal decrees, and contained numerous conflicting elements. Likewise, the political views of the Republican party or of the Democratic party do not comprise a unity. However, the system derived from John Calvin can claim such distinction.

Calvinism does not restrict itself to theology; it is an all-comprehensive system of thought, including views on politics, society, science, and art as well as theology. It presents a view of life and of the universe as a whole, a world- and lifeview. In fact, it has even been described as one of the few basic systems of thought that have ever been offered to man. James Orr limits the basic philosophic systems of the world to twelve, and considers all other philosophic systems to be modifications of these. Abraham Kuyper reduces the number of basic systems of thought to only four, of which Calvinism is one.

Calvinism Is Governed by a Fundamental Principle

Each unified system of thought is governed by an inherent fundamental principle or principles. This is also true of Calvinism. Beginning in the early nineteenth century, scholars, representing various schools of opinion, made a study to determine the genius of the Calvinistic movement.[2] Among these were scholars who had no eye for the organic unity within the system itself. They satisfied themselves with discovering some dominant trait which, in their estimation, set off Calvinism from other systems of thought. Thus, some characterized Calvinism as a religious system in which the spirit of democracy and the passion for liberty were distinguishing traits. This spirit was thought to have been derived from the liberty-loving Swiss among whom Calvinism arose. Others who had an eye for the legal aspects of the movement and the note of authority found in these the cardinal trait, and attributed it to the legal training of Calvin. Others considered the dominating characteristic to be the marvelous system which is peculiar to Calvinism. This was supposed to be due to Calvin's French temper of mind. Like the noted French military generals, he possessed the singular ability to marshal a stupendous array of facts, to organize and to mold them into one vast system. Others thought the prime factor of Calvinism to be its thorough break with the scholasticism of the Middle Ages, thus considering Calvin an advanced religious liberal. This trait was attributed to the humanistic training of his youth.

While these suggestions do contain grains of truth and do point to some marked feature in the system, none of them merits the distinction to be designated the dominant characteristic of Calvinism, much less its fundamental principle. William Hastie calls such suggestions "conjectures of ingenious thinkers inadequately acquainted with the conditions of the problem, rather than scientific conclusions derived from a full and exhaustive examination of the available material."[3] Those who have made exhaustive study of the problem will agree with Reinhold Seeberg that "this humanistically trained Frenchman was above all an evangelical Christian, and his whole world-view in the end was determined by his evangelical spirit."[4]

The fundamental principle, if anywhere, lies precisely in the field of the evangelical doctrines of the Calvinists conceived not as mere abstractions but as living, vital truths which motivated and dominated the whole of their lives. We may safely say that the fundamental principle concerns the doctrine of God. However scientific investigators may describe the fundamental principle of Calvinism, they are quite agreed with the philosopher Wilhelm Dilthey that the theological viewpoint is characteristic of the entire Calvinistic movement for the first 150 years, that the Calvinist of that time was always placing God at the center of his thoughts.[5] An examination of the Calvinistic confessions, especially those of early Reformation times, or of the works of Calvin will supply ample evidence of this.[6]

The central thought of Calvinism is, therefore, the great thought of God. Someone has remarked: "Just as the Methodist places in the foreground the idea of the salvation of sinners, the Baptist—the mystery of regeneration, the Lutheran—justification by faith, the Moravian—the wounds of Christ, the Greek Catholic—the mysticism of the Holy Spirit, and the Romanist—the catholicity of the church, so the Calvinist is always placing in the foreground the thought of God."[7] The Calvinist does not start out with some interest of man, for example, his conversion or his justification, but has as his informing thought always how will God come to his rights! He seeks to realize as his ruling concept in life the truth of Scripture: "Of him, and through him, and to him are all things. To whom be glory forever" (Rom. 11:36).

On this point there is widespread unanimity among the investigators. It is only when they proceed to express this idea in a definite formula that disagreements arise. Some have suggested that the attribute of God's self-existence (*aseitas*), as the most basic attribute we know in God, should be considered the fundamental principle of Calvinism. It is questionable whether the fundamental principle can be so stated; for it is not something in God, some specific attribute, that is basic to the system, but God himself. Moreover, the term "self-existence" does not express God's relation to the world outside of him, at least not directly; and, therefore, it can hardly be designated as the formative principle of a worldview which is to express this relation. God would be self-existent even if there were no world. Some term is needed which will express the relationship in which God stands to his created universe. The term which seems to indicate this relationship best, and is adopted by many, is "the absolute sovereignty of God," or more specifically, "the absolute sovereignty of God in the natural and the moral spheres."

The sense in which the term "sovereignty of God" is used needs to be well understood if it is to be safeguarded against gross misunderstanding. To the popular mind the term is likely to suggest that the Calvinist views God as a mere royal Ruler or Master who lays down the law to his creatures, and that the spirit of love in God and his grace and similar attributes are to be dissociated from the idea of his sovereignty. It is no surprise that some scholars like Albrecht Ritschl who have so interpreted the Calvinistic idea of the sovereignty of God suggest that the sovereignty of God is an inadequate fundamental principle for religion and that it ought to be superseded by the idea of the love of God. But certainly no good Calvinist would ever subscribe to such a limited view of God's sovereignty. Sovereignty is not even considered an attribute of God but a prerogative. What the Calvinist has in mind when he speaks of the sovereignty of God is something far broader than the idea that God is the Promulgator and Defender of the moral and physical laws of the universe. According to the Calvinist, God is not only the supreme Lawgiver and Ruler; but God is supreme also in the realm of truth, in science, and in art quite as much as in the realm of morals, in the dissemination of his love and grace and all his gifts, as well as in the administration of the laws which men are to live by or which operate in nature. The Calvinist believes that God does not act arbitrarily either in the dissemination of his gifts or in his providential control of man and nature. Order is heaven's first law. The realm of truth and of love, the scientific and the moral world, as well as the world of nature, is subject to law and order. The Calvinist observes in the universe created by God and maintained by his providence a beautiful system of law, order, and harmony, apparent in the realms of nature and grace, in the intellectual and moral life of men, in the distribution of all good—an all-pervasive system, all of God's making. In this distribution and administration of all things, God remains supreme. "Of him, and through him, and to him are all things."

When the term "sovereignty of God" is, accordingly, understood, not as a mere legalistic phrase indicative of God as the supreme Legislator and the One who has created the laws of nature, but in the more pregnant sense just described, there is nothing against the usage of the term to indicate thereby the fundamental principle of Calvinism. On the contrary, it would seem that it is then precisely the term to designate the absolute supremacy of God in all things and is, therefore, exactly the term to be used when we wish to construct a system with God at the center. This is precisely what the Calvinist has in mind when he employs the term. As the great Calvinist B. B. Warfield has expressed it: "From these things shine out upon us the formative principle of Calvinism. The Calvinist is the man who sees God behind all phenomena and in all that occurs recognizes the hand of God, working out His will; who makes the attitude of the soul to God in prayer its permanent attitude in all its life-activities; and who casts himself on the grace of God alone, excluding every trace of dependence on self from the whole work of his salvation."[8] The same author in another place asserts that the fundamental principle of Calvinism "lies in a profound apprehension of God in His majesty, with the inevitably accompanying poignant realization of the exact relation sustained to Him by the creature as such, and particularly by the sinful creature. . . . The Calvinist is the man who has seen God, and who, having seen God in His glory, is filled on the one hand with a sense of his own unworthiness to stand in God's sight as a creature, and much more as a sinner, and on the other with adoring wonder that nevertheless this God is a God Who receives sinners. He who believes in God without reserve, and is determined that God shall be God to him, in all his thinking, feeling, willing—in the entire compass of his life-activities, intellectual, moral, spiritual—throughout all his individual, social, religious relations—is by the force of the strictest of all logic which presides over the outworking of principles into thought and life, by the very necessity of the case, a Calvinist."[9]

With this description in mind it is easy to detect the fallacies in certain formulations of the fundamental principle of Calvinism. No statement of it is adequate which limits the supremacy of God in any way to certain spheres or to certain activities. It is a notable error to make the doctrine of election or predestination the fundamental principle. A popular notion that a Calvinist is a man who believes that God in a fatalistic way has decreed where man is to live in eternity must be dismissed immediately. As Charles Hodge has pointed out, the Calvinistic doctrine of predestination and fatalism agree in only one point: "Both assume absolute certainty in the sequence of all events. But they differ in the *ground* of this certainty, the *nature of the influence* by which it is secured, the *ends* contemplated, and the *effects* on the reason and the conscience of men."[10]

But even if we properly interpret predestination as the Calvinist would have us understand it, this doctrine could not be the fundamental principle of Calvinism. This is true for a variety of reasons. Predestination always concerns itself with man, with what is to become of him. It is not anything that may or may not happen to man that is fundamental to the Calvinist; it is the thought of the divine Being, his majesty, his greatness that primarily interests him. Furthermore, predestination treats only of God's activities with fallen man, and leaves out of consideration God's dealings with original man in the state of rectitude. It also limits God's activities to the world of moral beings, to men, and says nothing, at least not directly, about God's relationship to the world of nature. The Calvinist can know of no such limitation of the thought of God. He must place the idea of God in the foreground everywhere. From a theoretical point of view it is evident, therefore, that predestination cannot be considered the fundamental principle of Calvinism.

If we examine the Calvinistic confessions, especially the earlier ones drafted by Calvin or under his influence, or the *Institutes* of Calvin, we shall soon discover that predestination is not the fundamental principle. In some of these confessions the thought of predestination is not even as much as mentioned; in others it is cited only in passing. In the *Institutes* the doctrine of predestination is treated not as the basis of the system, but as a conclusion rather than as a premise in the soteriological section. It was only when the biblical doctrine of predestination was attacked by Pighuis that Calvin felt constrained to come to its defense in his treatises on "A Defense of the Secret Providence of God" and "The Eternal Predestination of God." Rather than call predestination the fundamental principle, it is more accurate to assert that predestination is a logical conclusion of Calvinism, or as E. Doumergue phrases it, the keystone rather than the foundation of the system.[11] When once you have adopted the view that God shall be God in the full sweep of his many relationships to his creatures, you will arrive at predestination as a very logical conclusion. All limitations of God's decree regarding man restrict God's supremacy and infringe upon his majesty.

The glory of God is another definition of the fundamental principle that has been proposed. It is a definition which is popular with the masses in Calvinistic circles. Calvinism has been defined as that system in which God is most highly glorified and man is most deeply abased. There is a very vital truth in this assertion. The Calvinist does make it an all-embracing purpose to glorify God in all walks of life. Nevertheless, as a definition this statement places too great a limitation upon the activity of God. The Calvinist is not only interested in including God in the purposes of life—living for his glory—but God is his first thought also when he thinks of the origin and providential control of all things. The purposive statement, the glory of God, is not sufficiently inclusive to be denominated the fundamental principle of Calvinism.

Some who have manifested deep concern for the responsibility of man and have feared that the emphasis on God's activity would crowd out the responsibility of man have proposed as the fundamental principle the combined thought of God's sovereign decree and the responsibility of man, since they saw in Calvinism an emphasis upon both factors. It is undoubtedly true that Calvinism does stress human responsibility to a very high degree. But again it would not be according to the genius of the Calvinist to place God's sovereign decree and man's responsibility, or any other aspect of man, on a level. God is to the Calvinist the first and last word, the primary thought always. God's sovereign decree and man's responsibility do present themselves to the human mind as an apparent contradiction, an antinomy, a paradox, something which the mind of man fails to comprehend. This paradox, like the one of God's transcendence and his immanence, or spirit and matter, the Calvinist readily adopts, even though he cannot understand it. However, he adopts this paradox not because he holds to two coequal fundamental principles—God's sovereignty and the freedom and responsibility of man—but because he wants to let God be God. He discovers that God in his written Word has stressed the responsibility of man, and that he is in no wise accountable for the sin of man, even though he is Ruler of all. It is just because the Calvinist would let God be God, that is, the final authority for his thinking, even when his own logic fails to give an adequate account of things, that he accepts the full responsibility of man, as God has informed him in his Word. The sovereignty of God, then, is prior to the responsibility of man.

Several other proposals have been made to designate the fundamental principle of Calvinism which need not be given special consideration here. No statement of the fundamental principle will be adequate which does not do full justice to the thought of God as the basic and central thought of Calvinism, since such a thought is by common consent its essence.

The Calvinistic System Is Based on This Principle

With the sovereignty of God in the natural and the moral spheres as fundamental principle, the Calvinist has built up his whole system. This has widespread implications for the views which the Calvinist entertains regarding theology, politics, sociology, science, and art—in fact the whole of life, as succeeding chapters will disclose.

Besides the fundamental principle there are corollary principles which should be mentioned here because they are, for the Calvinist, axiomatic principia, first principles which underlie the whole system. Of special prominence is the one which is familiarly known to us as the formal principle of the Protestant Reformation; namely, that God has given to fallen man, besides the general revelation in nature, a special revelation of himself and of his works in the Bible as the Word of God. Because this Bible, or rather God in the Bible, presents to us a specific interpretation of God's works in nature and a special revelation of his redemptive works, it becomes for the Calvinist the ultimate and binding source of information concerning God and the world. This objective revelation man accepts through a God-given faith.

The Bible, as revelation of God, teaches the following facts of basic significance to the Calvinistic system: that God, who has revealed himself in his Word, is sovereign over all things, and that God differs essentially from all things created by him; that religion, or the relation of God to his image-bearer, man, is of the nature of a covenant, and as such was already specially revealed to original man in the state of righteousness; that the world today does not exist in a pure state but is fallen in sin. Furthermore, regarding the fallen world, the Bible maintains that man is totally depraved and that the world, over which God placed him as ruler, exists today in a corrupt state as a result of sin; that death has come into the world as a punishment for sin; and that the sovereign God has revealed his grace, which affects both individual and social conditions, in the divinely given Mediator, Jesus Christ.[12] What hypotheses are to a philosophic system, these facts derived from Scripture are to the Calvinistic system; they underlie and control that system in its many ramifications.

2

The Place of the Bible

If God is the all-controlling thought in the Calvinistic system, then it is only natural that the Calvinist will want to see all things as God wants him to see them and aim to carry out God's will in all things. From this fact one can readily infer what place the Bible will occupy in the system and the life of the Calvinist. He will make God's Word the canon, which means the rule, for his life. It will be the rule of faith (which guides his intellect) and practice (which determines his daily duty).

The First and Original Revelation of God Was Nature

In reality God has given two books, two revelations of himself: the book of nature and the book of Scripture. Although as revelations from God these two books are not equal, as we shall see presently, it is an important Calvinistic principle to hold to both nature and Scripture as revelations from God. Some maintain that only nature is the book of God and ignore the Bible as a special revelation; others go to the opposite extreme and ignore nature as a revelation from God. The Calvinist accepts both. A few, like the Roman Catholics and the Quakers, are inclined to add something as a special revelation to the Bible, either a church decree, or pronouncement of the pope, or some revelation which the Christian is supposed to receive.

By the book of nature the Calvinist understands more than the mere natural objects of God's creation such as minerals, flora, fauna, and men. These natural objects were not only created by God, but he also directs them in their movements in history. Therefore, history, both natural and human, reveals to us many facts about God and shows us his finger. In addition to nature and history, moreover, we must also include man himself. The psalmist once said, "I am fearfully and wonderfully made" (Ps. 139:14). Man himself as the image of God tells us much about God.

This book of nature tells us not only about natural objects themselves and their history; it is God's book, in which the Calvinist sees spread out before him God's ideas, something of his excellence and of his will. He deems it his duty to read this book of nature, to study it, and to think God's thoughts after him. This is all the more necessary because these thoughts are not arranged in a ready-made system but are imbedded in nature. God wants his creature to discover these ideas, find their unity and harmony, their essential nature and purpose. Thus, it can be seen how broad a view of life the Calvinist must take. He considers it his duty to investigate all of life and, as a matter of intellectual culture, to develop these implicit ideas, fit them into a harmonious, explicit whole, and use them for his God. If his God has given him the book of nature to study, the Calvinist must develop a world- and lifeview. The whole of nature and all of life become a sacred court wherein he honors God.

The Second Revelation of God Was the Bible

But God also has another book, the Bible. Originally there was only one book, one revelation of God, namely, nature. And in the next world there will again be only one book, the new nature, in which man will see God and his revealed will. Adam saw, and redeemed man in eternity will see, God's will clearly revealed in his heart and in nature round about him, and will, therefore, have no need of a special revelation in a Bible.

That fact accounts for the existence of the second book, the Bible, or the special revelation as we have it today. This book became necessary because of sin. When man fell, both he and nature changed. Man's mind became darkened so that he could not see things as they are; and nature was distorted, as the statement in Genesis about "thorns and thistles" suggests. Nature today still is a mirror in which the virtues of God are reflected, but because of sin it has become a decidedly curved mirror. Manifestly, a curved mirror makes things look grotesque, very different from what they actually are. How now is man with his beclouded mind and distorted nature to know God and the universe aright, or to know his true nature and the purpose of his existence? These are three fundamental questions at the basis of his whole outlook upon the world.

How is man to obtain the proper insight into ultimate issues under such conditions? The only solution is that God give him another book, the Bible, in which he clearly and unerringly reveals the truth about these matters to man, and then enlighten man's darkened mind by his Holy Spirit, so that he will be able to understand this biblical truth.

Thus we see the relation in which the Bible stands to the book of nature. The Bible is not on a level with nature as a revelation of God, but it is rather a corrective of false impressions made by nature in its distorted condition. It presents to us views about God and the universe which nature today does not teach properly. As Calvin states, we must look at nature through the spectacles of the Bible. So then, while God has indeed two revelations which he calls upon his creature to study, the Bible after all becomes the ultimate basis for the whole view of life for the Christian, since he needs the biblical outlook to properly interpret nature and life round about him.

However, the Bible does more than act as interpreter of nature, since it also contains a special revelation of salvation for the sinner. This important information nature cannot give us, for the simple reason that nature was already created before there was a way of salvation open to sinners. How, then, could nature tell us anything about it? Yet the salvation of man is in fact the central theme of the Bible and is inseparably bound up with the view which it presents of the universe and of human life.

Do not mistake the purpose of the Bible as if it were intended to be a textbook for the various sciences. It is not intended as such. One gathers the facts for the various sciences from the fields which he is investigating—nature, history, psychology, and related studies. However, when the student proceeds to interpret and correlate these facts, relating the truths of any particular science to the whole body of knowledge, then he needs the unifying interpretation of Scripture. We cannot have a proper view of God, the universe, man, or history without the Bible.

This book, therefore, besides teaching us the way of salvation, provides us with the principles which must govern the whole of our life, including our thinking as well as our moral conduct. Not only science and art, but our homelife, our business, and our social and political problems must be viewed and solved in the light of scriptural truth and fall under its direction.

This is even true of philosophy. It might be supposed that since philosophy is the science of fundamentals, that Christian philosophy will have to base itself ultimately upon reason and try to explain all problems in philosophy upon a purely rationalistic basis without accepting Bible testimony as final; but even here the Calvinist does not base his acceptance of Bible truths upon his philosophy, but, rather, he begins with the basic truths of the Bible as his foundation. His is specifically a philosophy based on revelation. Just as all philosophic systems start out with their unproved basic assumptions or hypotheses, so the Christian starts out with the truths of revelation as his basic assumptions. The Calvinistic procedure is not the Bible based on philosophy, but Christian philosophy based upon the Bible.

The principles for faith and life which the Bible embodies, as well as the truths of the way of salvation, are presented to us in historic forms and are linked up with what the Bible relates of the history of men and of nations. Hence, it is to be expected that not all of what the Bible teaches is equally important, and not all can be considered a rule for our life. Some facts are recorded in it which are the very opposite of a rule of life, as when Absalom shamefully mistreated his father David. Other parts of Scripture contain regulations which are not intended to be for all ages but only for a specific occasion or period. Thus, Calvin calls attention to the fact that several of the civil laws of Moses were not intended for today at all but were only of temporary significance. But the Bible presents the underlying rules of life, the eternal principles, in the light of which it views the history it records and according to which it intends that we order our lives. These eternal principles are found not only in the New Testament but in the Old as well.

The Bible Is the Calvinist's Rule for Thought and Action

The Calvinist holds the authority of the Bible to be absolute. He does not consider the Bible to be just so much good advice which a man is free to follow in case he finds it expedient and which he is free to ignore if he pleases. The Bible is for him an absolute rule before which he must bow unfailingly. It dictates to him what he must believe and what he must do. It comes to him with commanding force. Calvin was very insistent on this point. If the Bible had spoken, there was only one thing to do—obey.

The explanation of this high regard for the Bible lay, of course, in the consideration that it was the Word of God. Because God had spoken and had given in it the revelation of his will for our lives, therefore, it was to be obeyed. For the Calvinist the Bible is not, as it is for the modernist, the personal interpretation of religion and life by religious geniuses. Back of the writers of the Bible the Calvinist saw the unerring hand of God. When he reflected upon how men wrote the Bible, he insisted that they were organically (not mechanically) inspired, meaning that God used these men with all their talents and led them to write just as he wanted, so that the product was his thoughts. And when the Calvinist contemplated the contents of the Bible, he said it was verbally, as well as factually, inspired. And when he thought of the purpose which God had in mind when he caused these men to write, he said it was a plenary inspiration, that is, an inspiration which directed them to include completely all that God had intended.

An important question arises here. How does the Calvinist know that the Bible is the Word of God? On what does the Calvinist ground his belief that the Bible is God's book? This is a very important question and will be considered in the discussion of the next topic, the place of faith.

3

The Place of Faith

A modernist, one who denies the specifically supernatural, does not have much room for faith in God. For the Calvinist, faith in God will occupy a very large, in fact, a determinative place in his life. These two systems are just about opposite poles, and this is seen very clearly in their attitude to faith.

Faith Occupies an Important Place in Calvinism

The following will illustrate. Modernists are generally recognized by one outstanding characteristic. They frequently differ from one another in all sorts of detail; one modernist often denies what another affirms. But they all agree in this one particular: they all deny the specifically supernatural, such as miracles, special revelation and inspiration, the virgin birth, the bodily resurrection (either of Christ or of believers), special answers to prayer, and any operation of God apart from the laws of nature and the normal operations of human life. To many of them there is not even a supernatural God, who is a person, who thinks and wills apart from man, who can hear you when you pray. God is merely an impersonal power in the universe. If you so believe, what benefit will faith in God have for you? He cannot hear you. Certainly, nothing out of the ordinary will ever happen to you, even if you do pray. What the pantheistic modernist means by faith in God when he so speaks amounts to this: Have faith in the divine in yourself, that is, have self-confidence, since you are a part of God.

Moreover, the modernist cannot have faith in the Bible as God's special revelation; for to him the Bible is not God's revelation but the product of what religious men of former days have thought about God and about religious things. Then why, if it is not God's revelation, make the Bible the foundation of what you believe about the basic problems of the universe? Extract from the writings of the Bible whatever sounds reasonable to you and omit the rest. Rely upon your own reason, not upon faith in what the authors of the Bible say. In such a creed there is obviously little room for faithful trust in God, either in his revelation concerning the ultimate problems of life or in his providence in the hour of dire need. The best thing a modernist can do is to rely upon himself, upon his own insight and natural powers.

Now turn to the Calvinist position. Here you have the very opposite viewpoint. The Calvinist believes in a supernatural God who reveals himself not only in nature but also in specifically supernatural acts, such as biblical revelation and inspiration; who daily provides qualifying strength to those who ask, and regenerates and sanctifies by special acts of his Holy Spirit. In such a system there is much to be gained from believing and trusting in God. If the Calvinist wishes to know about the fundamental problems of life or the world, he can trust the special revelation which his God gives him for information and guidance. And if he needs moral power, he can call upon God who gives him grace for help in time of need. Even in nature, then, there is the intelligent, purposeful leadership of a personal God, directing man's life and all things, not as an impersonal force but as a wise and good heavenly Father.

Moreover, the need of faith in God for the Calvinist becomes all the more necessary, because he believes man's mind to be darkened by sin and his soul morally depraved, not partially but totally; that is, the depraved condition reaches out over his whole nature. In his depraved condition, therefore, man cannot have the proper intellectual insight or moral power, but must rely upon God's special grace for both thought and walk. The Calvinist has caught the great meaning of such biblical phrases as "Through faith we understand that the worlds were framed by the word of God, so that things which are seen were not made of things which do appear" (Heb. 11:3); "Without Me ye can do nothing" (John 15:5); "I can do all things through

Christ which strengtheneth me" (Phil. 4:13). The Calvinistic system, as you will notice, roots itself in faith throughout. "We believe in order that we may know," and "we believe in order that we may achieve a life worthwhile for God."

But here an important question arises! Can you build a system upon such a faith and still be considered scientific? The modernist claims that you cannot; the Calvinist maintains that you can. Some religious groups have separated religion and science altogether and do not even try to harmonize them. The problem deserves far broader discussion that we can devote to it here. But we can perhaps gain some understanding of it by contrasting briefly a method commonly defended by modernists as the means of arriving at scientific knowledge in religion with the approach employed by Calvinists.

Is Faith in the Supernatural Scientifically Defensible?

Modernists did not impugn the position of orthodox Christians because they considered them insufficiently pious. The main objection was rather that they were not scientific. To be scientific one should follow an altogether different method than the one of faith in a supernatural revelation. To be scientific a person should in the study of religion advance by the same method that is followed in the natural sciences, for example, physics or chemistry. First he must gather from experience all the data he can that have anything to do with religion. Then he must group all similar facts and classify them. Obviously one cannot examine God by this method, for he is not a fact of observation. But he can study manifestations of religion in this world, religious persons, and religious documents wherever he finds them, in Christian or in pagan lands. After the student has gathered these facts and classified them, he eliminates the essential from the nonessential; and thus, it is said, the searcher will arrive at the genuine in religion in a purely inductive, scientific fashion. The result will be a scientifically defensible religion.

The method might appeal to some at first sight as being an excellent one with which to arrive at scientific results in religion. But those who have tried to construct a scientific religion by this method, as has Ernst Troeltsch and his school of positivists in Germany, have come to most disappointing results. When they finally presented what they thought to be scientifically established truth in religion, the product was so meager that it could hardly be called a religion, surely not one that a man could live by. All that they secured was vague notions about God, about the problem of evil, and about heaven and hell. That was substantially all that they thought they could prove by this method.

But there are not only objections to the results which the method yielded, but to the method itself. It does not, as it claims to do, establish a religion upon a purely experiential basis of facts. Suppose one gathers all the religious data available from contemporary religious manifestation and suppose one classifies such data as well as he can; yet, sooner or later, he will have to sift the essential from the nonessential. He will have to determine what is genuine religion and what is not. To do this one will have to apply some standard. Note carefully that that standard is never going to be the result or part of the method employed but will exist independently of it. One man will, for example, say the genuine in religion consists in one thing, another in something else. Thus, to call attention to some general standards, certain scholars will say that religion is essentially intellectual; others, that it is essentially emotional; still others, that it is essentially volitional. All these estimates of what religion really is are not the products of those investigations of the religious phenomena, but are presumptions, hypotheses, notions about the nature of religion which a person has apart from the investigation. Thus, when the scholar arrives at the end of his investigation and is to tell us what religion really is, he judges it by a standard which itself is not a result of his investigations. His view of religion is based on his assumptions, and his method does not build up a religious view which is scientific in the sense that it has no assumptions.

Do not judge the modernists too harshly for this. While they cannot make good their claim to give us a religion without assumptions, they are doing what every school of thought is doing right along. All have their basic unproven presuppositions, their working hypotheses. The only man who has no basic assumptions is the skeptic, and he gets nowhere. The Greeks already knew this. Plato built his school on his basic assumptions. When Aristotle could not agree with the basic assumptions of Plato, he originated a school with his own basic assumptions as its foundation. And the modernist, with all his high claims, is no different in this respect than the Calvinist. Both have their basic presuppositions. The Calvinist has them in the fundamental tenets of his faith based on the revelation in the Bible, while the modernist has them in his basic hypotheses.

Another objection to the modernist is that he does not even consistently apply his method of investigation. Whenever he finds in history a fact asserted to be miraculous, he brushes it aside with the claim that miracles cannot occur. But that is just the point at issue. When he meets with such a well-established historical fact as the resurrection of Christ or the revelation to the prophets, the thing to do, to be scientific, is to accept the facts, even though they clash with some theory. When Friedrich Delitzsch was once asked why he, as a brilliant scholar, joined the orthodox ranks, he replied, "The resurrection of Jesus Christ is a fact." If certain miracles do occur, it is the duty of a scientific man to accept them and incorporate them in his theory.

But, what is more important, it is not true that the only method by which to arrive at truth in religion is the one followed in the natural sciences. In the sciences of the spirit (so-called *Geisteswissenschaften*) we arrive at knowledge by reason, not by observation. There is still a third avenue by which we arrive at truth, and that is by faith. We are all using this approach in by far the greatest amount of knowledge we receive. Most of our knowledge comes to us, not through our own observation, or from reasoning it out for ourselves, but through the testimony of reliable authorities. In religion the Calvinist is doing this very thing when he accepts the divine revelation given in the Bible on the strength of the authority of God. It is often asserted that it is scientifically impossible to have a special revelation from God. Yet that depends upon the kind of God one has. Science itself does not and cannot disprove the possibility of a special revelation from a personal God. If a human personality can impose himself upon this natural world without disturbing the normal operation of mechanical laws, why can a personal God not do the same thing, and thereby give us his revelation? It is unscientific not to accept that possibility.

If God has given us a revelation of himself and in it has explained to man the basic problems of the universe, its origin, nature, and destiny, then we have in that divine revelation a veritable gold mine of truth which cannot be ignored except at the greatest cost.

How Can the Christian Know That Scripture Is God's Word?

How can we know that God has given us a revelation of himself and of the universe—its origin, nature, and destiny—and that this revelation is to be found in the Christian Bible?

This question is an age-old one, and men have used various methods to answer it. One method, akin to the inductive method of natural science followed by many today, is the comparative study of religions. Some think that by placing the religious books of the world side by side, one can come to a conclusion as to which of these contains the best and truest form of religion. But to arrive at such a conclusion one will have to use some standard. And the conclusion arrived at will depend upon the standard used. Not all investigators have decided in favor of the Christian religion. On the other hand, it is true that most scholars in Christian lands have adjudged the Christian religion peerless. Certainly, no one with an enlightened Christian conscience need fear that upon investigation of these religious systems he will not find that the Christian Bible stands miles higher than all religious books in its views of God, the origin and nature of things, the cause of evil, redemption from evil, and life beyond the grave. While this much satisfaction may be gained from a comparative study of religions, one will have difficulty in arriving by this method at the conviction which the Christian religion requires, namely, that it alone is true.

Another method is that of Christian apologetics and Christian evidences. This method searches out the arguments which can be advanced to prove that the Christian God is the true God, that the Bible is his revelation, and that the Christian religion is the true religion. There are many diverse arguments one might advance to prove that the Bible is God's Word. One might mention, as people commonly do, that the revelation in the Bible when given by God was time and again accompanied by supernatural signs and wonders, thus proving its supernatural source—for instance, when great disturbances in nature accompanied the giving of the law on Mount Sinai, or when men saw the signs and wonders which accompanied Christ's message, or his birth and his resurrection. Again, one might point out that the Bible discloses facts that God alone can know: the creation of the world, prediction of future events which have come to pass, and lofty thoughts which convince us of the divine origin of the Bible. Furthermore, the divine library of sixty-six books in the Bible was written by about forty different human authors in the space of 1,600 years, and yet the Bible presents to us an amazing unity, which indicates that there must have been a Master Mind controlling those human minds. Or one might point to the way in which archeological research in recent years is presenting a remarkable witness to the great accuracy of the biblical record of historic events. Attention might be directed to the transcendent concepts of the Bible and the great moral influence it has exerted upon the lives of men as no human book has been able to do, indicating that it must be more than a merely human book.

The Bible itself at times makes use of the apologetic method. When Elijah on Mount Carmel stated that the God who would answer by fire was to be considered the true God, he was making use of the apologetic method. And when Moses in Deuteronomy 18:22 calls attention to the fulfilment of a prophecy as evidence of its genuineness, he is using an apologetic argument. And when our Lord appeals to the unbelieving Jews to believe him "for the very works' sake," and when it is said that though he did many miracles among them, yet they believed not, the appeal is of the apologetic type. The fact that the Bible repeatedly uses this argument proves that the method has relative value and may be used by us in combating opponents. The truth is that the Christian religion can by apologetics present a strong case to prove that it is more reasonable to believe what the Christian religion teaches than to believe the opposite. The apologetic arguments also give to the believer himself abundant proof of the reasonableness of his faith.

We should, however, be on our guard not to expect too much from the apologetic method, rational arguments for the existence of God, or proofs that the Bible is the Word of God. In the case of all such sciences as ethics, law, esthetics, philosophy, and religion, where the final decision rests upon the individual's own evaluation, there is always room for wide divergence of opinion. The fool can always say in his heart, "There is no God." While a Christian can prove that his Christian position is fully as reasonable as the opponent's view, there is no such thing as an absolutely compelling proof to which an unbeliever will yield. No one can produce completely convincing proof that God exists, or that the Bible is the Word of God, just as little as anyone can prove their opposites.

There is still a third way by which the Christian can come to know that the Bible is the Word of God. This is by the method of faith. In fact, this is the basic method used by the Christian. In the last analysis the Christian does not base his belief in God and God's Word on rational arguments. No matter how many or how excellent the arguments he may be able to advance that he has the correct view, the Christian has not been led to accept the Bible as God's Word after working his way through a maze of puzzling questions about whether God exists or whether the Bible is the Word of God. Even if the Christian should by rational argumentation come to the conclusion that the Bible is God's Word, that would give him at best historical but not saving faith. It is one thing to say, "Taking all things into consideration, I come to the conclusion that God exists"; it is quite another to affirm with the Christian: "I believe in God the Father, Maker of heaven and earth." Christian faith does not rest on its own reasoning but in God. Christian faith is in this respect simply a God-implanted conviction in the soul that the Bible is the Word of God. Like all faith it is intuitive, coming directly to the soul and so overpowering it with the conviction that the Bible is God's Word that the person cannot refuse to believe it.

How Does the Spirit Testify to the Christian?

This conviction implanted in the soul we call the testimony of the Holy Spirit in the heart of the believer. It is of importance to have clearly before our minds just wherein this testimony of the Holy Spirit consists. It might be supposed that what the Holy Spirit does is simply to enlighten our minds so that we come to see things in a different light, and that this new insight then leads us to accept the Bible as the Word of God. In that case you will notice that our enlightened reason—enlightened by the Holy Spirit, but still our reason—lies at the basis of our acceptance of the Bible as God's Word. Note that we then would still basically be rationalists. We then believe what we can prove with our enlightened reason.

The following considerations, however, make such a conclusion impossible on a Calvinistic basis. First of all, faith is intuitional; it is a conviction which is not the result of a process of discursive reasoning, but something which comes directly or immediately to the soul. Insofar, however, it might still be reasoning. Aristotle distinguishes between two kinds of reason: that which is by the process of intellectual argumentation and that which is by immediate insight.

But faith is not only something immediate and direct. It accepts something as true, not on the basis of a person's own insight, but on the basis of the testimony of another, in this case the testimony of God. No matter how much insight may or may not be accompanied with it, faith always rests upon the testimony of God, not upon the believer's own insight.

Again, saving faith differs from faith in general or historical faith in this important aspect, that it implies, besides an intellectual agreement to a proposition, an element of personal trust. It roots itself in God.

We can perhaps best summarize what the testimony of the Holy Spirit in the heart of the believer amounts to in the following negative and positive propositions. The testimony of the Holy Spirit does not lie in the fact that he gives the believer some new heavenly revelation, some new thought in addition to the Bible. Nor does it consist in the fact that he leads the believer to conclude as a result of illuminated reason and rational argumentation that the Bible is God's Word; nor in the fact that he leads the believer through an experience of the power of the Bible to conclude that it is God's book. But it consists in the fact that he leads the believer freely and spontaneously to acknowledge the divine authority which the Bible itself claims to have and everywhere demands, which makes the Christian submit to the Bible as God's Word. In a word, he impresses upon the soul of the Christian the fact of the divineness of the Bible, or, to use the Latin term which has been employed, the *divinitas* of the Bible.[1] The Christian then accepts the Bible as true on the strength of this conviction. If you should try to find the root of that conviction and ask why the Christian believes that the Bible is that divine book and why he thus places his trust in God, then, to use a phrase of Herman Bavinck, the Christian must acknowledge that he is unable to give the answer.[2] In other words, this is an axiom, a fundamental truth with the Christian.

After the Christian has thus been convinced of the divineness of the Bible through the Holy Spirit's testimony in the heart, he may, and no doubt will, with his enlightened mind illumined by the Holy Spirit, also see things in a different light and will adopt many arguments advancing the reasonableness of accepting the Bible as the Word of God. But no Christian ever *grounds* his faith upon these arguments. The ancient church fathers like Augustine and Anselm were right when they said that *fides precedit intellectum* ("faith precedes intelligence").

Remember, too, that the Holy Spirit by his testimony in the heart does not change the Bible into a thoroughly demonstrable book, which you can prove from the first verse to the last. For several reasons this is impossible because of the very nature of the case. In such sciences as law, psychology, esthetics, philosophy, or theology so many things depend upon personal judgments—which differ with different individuals—that you cannot prove your point in a positivistic way as in mathematics. Also, much of what the Bible teaches lies beyond our observation and reason, such as the accounts of creation or the future world. Again, much of what the Bible teaches, though not antirational (against reason) is yet suprarational (above reason); for example, the doctrines of the Trinity or the virgin birth. So then there will always remain much that is fundamental in biblical teaching that you will accept not because your enlightened reason proves to you that it is true, but simply because you accept God's testimony that it is as he has stated in his Word. For your consolation remember that no one can properly object to your position as being unscientific because you accept some basic positions which you cannot prove. For every philosophic system does the same thing when it, too, starts out with its basic assumptions, its own working hypotheses, which it cannot prove. If you are unscientific in starting out with such assumptions, then all others are likewise.

In conclusion, let me point to the importance of this position and its harmony with the best thought of historic Christianity by quoting a statement of William G. T. Shedd, well-known professor of systematic theology at Union Theological Seminary in New York City. Speaking of faith and science, he remarked:

> As we follow the history of Apologetics down to the present day, we perceive that leading minds have been supernaturalists or rationalists in their methods of defending and philosophizing upon Christianity, according as they have adopted or rejected the dictum first announced by Origen, repeated by Augustine, and most thoroughly expanded and established by Anselm—the dictum, *fides precedit intellectum* (faith precedes intelligence). In the former class, we find the names of Origen, Augustine, Anselm, Calvin, Pascal. In the latter, the names of men like Scotus Erigena, Abelard, Raymond Lully, in whom the speculative energy overmastered the contemplative, and whose intuition and construction of Christian Doctrine was inadequate, and in some instances, certainly, fatally defective.[3]

4

The Balance of the System

In studying the Calvinistic religion one is immediately impressed by the proper balance in the emphasis placed upon the several doctrines which the Calvinist believes.

Reasons for Calvinism's Balance

In not a few theological circles one will discover an emphasis upon a certain truth out of all proportion to other truths. Thus the Methodist of a generation ago emphasized conversion, the Baptists, baptism, the premillennialist of today emphasizes the second coming of Christ, and the modern religious liberal, social service. The Calvinist acknowledges that all these matters of belief just cited are important elements of the Christian religion, but he does not stress any one at the expense of the others. There is a very definite reason for this. When you take as the central thought in your religion some fact, let us say, conversion or baptism or justification by faith, which concerns only man's salvation, the proper balance in your theology is lost. But when you place at the center of your system, as the Calvinist does, the great thought of God as the Sovereign of the universe, then everything can fall into its proper place and receive its due share of emphasis.

But there is another reason why Calvinism is able to maintain a proper balance. It is the fact that the Calvinist does not hesitate to include in his theological beliefs ideas which are logical opposites, that is, ideas which seem to be in direct conflict, paradoxes. The Calvinist has the reputation of being a strong logical reasoner; nevertheless, because he makes the Bible his ultimate foundation, he does not hesitate to include in his system ideas difficult for reason to harmonize, ideas which seem to be logical opposites, as long as his Bible gives him reason for so doing.

Examples of Calvinism's Balance

This fact is of great importance. It keeps the Calvinist from becoming a one-sided extremist. A few examples may serve as illustrations. Take the seemingly logical opposites of predestination and human responsibility. John Calvin and Calvinists believe wholeheartedly in absolute predestination. But nowhere do you find human responsibility stressed more emphatically than in Calvin's writings and among Calvinists. If you should ask the Calvinist, "But how do you harmonize these two?" he would reply, "That is unnecessary! God reconciles them, and that is enough for me." While he can illuminate this harmony to a certain extent, basically it is a mystery and he is content to let it be so.

Or take these two opposites: the doctrine of election, which stresses God's activity, and the covenant of grace as a responsibility, which stresses man's activity. Although the study presents problems, there is no group that maintains both as ardently as does the Calvinist.

Again, reflect upon these facts which to some appear as opposites, namely, sin and grace as they affect man. There is no system that puts man the sinner down so low as does the Calvinist with his doctrine of total depravity. But there is none that places the Christian on a higher pedestal or demands more of him than does this same Calvinist.

You might adduce the eternal conflict about the relation between spirit and matter. The materialist is always trying to reduce spirit to matter. The idealistic pantheist maintains that matter arose from spirit. The Calvinist does not hesitate to accept the dualism of matter and spirit. He maintains that these are distinct substances, created by the same God, but as distinct from one another as they are from God the Creator.

Another apparent conflict is the one between separation

from the world and culture. Whereas the secular man feels nothing for separation from the world, some Christians lay all stress on separation from the world but do not realize their calling to share in the cultural development of the world and their duty to be a leaven in human society. The Calvinist keeps his equilibrium by stressing both as the Bible demands.

As a last example we call attention to the contrast between intellectualism and mysticism. Men are inclined to be either one-sidedly intellectual or emotional in their religious life. One of the very best tributes paid to Calvin and the Calvinistic movement in this respect is that they have been called by some intellectualists, by others mystics, and by still others voluntarists who stress the will in religion. Certainly Calvinists must be balanced Christians if they can be charged with stressing all three. It is needless to say that Calvinists have not always fulfiled the demands of Calvinism. They have at times been one-sided, stressing either the intellect or the will or the emotions. But in so doing they have not practiced a full-orbed Calvinism, which provides for a proper emphasis on all three.

Calvinism in history proved itself to be a system of great energy. It might easily, therefore, have gone off on a tangent in one direction or another had it not readily incorporated into the system these complementary opposites. It was thereby kept from radical one-sidedness and was able to maintain its balance.

5

The Main Theological Tenets

The foregoing discussion has focused on matters which concern the Calvinistic movement as a whole. We can now proceed to Calvinistic principles in their more detailed application to such specific fields as religion, politics, society, art, and related subjects.

We shall begin with religion. We need not attempt to enumerate the many principles which apply to this field. Those who desire information about Calvinistic principles as they apply to religion can find abundant material at their disposal in the works on Reformed dogmatics by such leading theologians as Abraham Kuyper, Herman Bavinck, Charles Hodge, Geerhardus Vos, and Louis Berkhof. I may be permitted to refer to two compendiums in which one will find excellent summaries of the Calvinistic principles in the field of theology. The one is by L. Berkhof, *Manual of Reformed Doctrine*; the other is by A. A. Hodge, *Outlines of Theology* (rewritten and enlarged). We shall devote our discussion only to the outstanding characteristics of the Calvinistic religion.

God and the Bible

If there is one Christian who stresses belief in God, it is the Calvinist. His first and last thought everywhere is God. This is the golden thread that colors the whole of Calvinistic theology. Everything depends upon God. Religion, although it blesses man, exists not for man, but in the last analysis for God. "Of him, and through him, and to him are all things."

Consider the Calvinist's view regarding the universe of created things! Not only does he believe that it was created by God; but all that occurs in it, whether in nature or in human life, he holds to be but the unfolding of the divine plan of the ages. Even sin does not happen as an accident. God willingly permitted sin, lets it work according to its own inherent nature, and controls it for his own glory. God works upon this creation in either of two ways. He works through the normal operations of the universe. Men, even sinful men, and nature act freely according to their own impulses or laws. They are, however, only the secondary causes; behind them lies God, as the First Cause of all things. He, without compelling any secondary causes to act contrary to their own nature and choice, brings to pass all that happens in the universe. The second method by which God operates upon this world is by miracles: special revelation, inspiration, wonders, incarnation, physical resurrection, regeneration, and sanctification. The Calvinist does not rest content, whether he views the normal operations of nature or God's special, miraculous revelations, until he has traced all events back to God and dedicated them to him.

The same prominence given to this great idea of God meets us in the Calvinist's attitude toward the Bible. It is not only the book that tells the Calvinist how to be saved. It is to him the book of God, who speaks to him on every page and tells him of his plans and purposes as these relate to his salvation, and also to his duty in every domain of life.

Mankind

When you come to the study of man, again it is the same thought of God that colors it. Even unfallen man, compared to the majestic God, is as less than nothing and vanity. Whole nations are accounted as the small dust of the balance. Unfallen man is already absolutely dependent upon God. How much more fallen man? He is totally depraved, unable to do any good and inclined to all wickedness. Either through external compulsion as of governments, or fear of punishment or public opinion, or selfish considerations that it pays to do good, or love of those that love him, sinful man is led by God's common grace to do things which his evil-inclined heart would not otherwise want to do. These restraints and the promptings to do things for the good of human society are not due to any good in natural man but to the common grace of God. Thus, whatever good you see anywhere in the world, in society, art, science, political life, even in pagan lands, the Calvinist ascribes directly to God as its source, not to the sinful heart of man.

Furthermore, this sad condition of man's total depravity cannot be altered except by a supernatural change wrought by God. Man is as enslaved to his sinful habits as a drunkard to drink, so that he cannot and will not turn to God of himself. "It is God which worketh in you both to will and to do of his good pleasure."

Make a careful study of the redemption through Christ, and you will find the same prominence given to the thought of God. The plan of redemption did not originate in the mind of man, for man would not have turned to God of himself. It was planned by God. The Savior is God-given. Moreover, Jesus did not earn only such portions of our salvation as we could not earn. We could not earn a thing. Nor did he atone for whatever we could not atone for. He did it all. Jesus did all the obeying that was necessary to gain eternal life for us. And he suffered all the punishment that was necessary to remove the guilt of sin. Salvation thereby becomes purely a God-given blessing of free grace without any merit on our part.

Let us develop this further. One might say, *God planned salvation, and he earned it in Christ.* Now the choice of acceptance or rejection is mine alone. In a sense it is so. But who causes a Christian to accept Christ? "For we are all gone astray. There is none that seeketh after God." So Christ sends the Holy Spirit into our stubborn hearts, regenerates us, and puts faith and love to God there, as well as new ambitions and desires. This he does with irresistible power—not, as the Arminians say, if we let him; we would never spontaneously let him. We only work out our own salvation because it is God that worketh in us, both to will and do of his good pleasure. Thus the entire work of redemption in its essentials is the work of God. God the Father planned it. God the Son earned it. And God the Holy Spirit applies it, regenerating heart and life. While the modernist attributes the whole of man's salvation to his own efforts, and the Arminian ascribes only part of it to God and the remainder to man, the Calvinist ascribes to God all the glory. Even all man's achievements in accepting salvation are of him.

The Church and the Spirit

Another outstanding doctrine, much discussed in the early history of Calvinism in its conflict with Roman Catholicism, is the doctrine of the church. Study the Calvinist view with regard to the church, and the emphasis on God again becomes very apparent. The Roman Catholic seemingly begins at the same point as the Calvinist when it concerns matters of supernatural salvation, placing them all in God's hand. The Roman Catholic believes that in natural things man can do all manner of good in purely Pelagian fashion, but that for supernatural salvation he is totally dependent upon God. Moreover, he inserts the priest between God and man as the dispenser of salvation. The pope is Christ's vicar, his substitute on earth. He wears the papal tiara, or triple crown, to indicate that he is ruler over the church, over the state, and over the region of purgatory. The church distributes salvation through the sacraments. If you desire removal of original sin, you get it from the church in the sacrament of baptism; forgiveness of daily sins is secured by penance or confession to the priest; spiritual strengthening is afforded by mass; and the like. You are made dependent upon the church for your salvation throughout. Even to acquire a true knowledge of the way of salvation, you cannot go to the Bible directly, but the church must interpret it for you.

Where the Roman Catholic places the church, the Calvinist places God the Holy Spirit. He enlightens the mind so that the renewed man himself has sufficient clearness to know the way of salvation by the study of the Bible. And the Christian receives from the Holy Spirit directly such grace as is acquired, according to the Roman Catholics, only through the instituted channel of the church. The church itself is not identified with any special denomination or set of officials, but is the body of true believers of all times and places, who are the body of Christ and as such are empowered to elect their own officers when organizing in any given locality into a local church.

The government of the church is another important element in Calvinism to which the fundamental principle of the sovereignty of God gives a distinctive coloring. It does so especially in two respects, that of authority and that of liberty. Because Christ is head of the church, he is its rightful and only Sovereign to whose wishes all in the church must conform. The church is, therefore, to be organized as it was in the apostolic era. Discipline is to be administered not merely to rid the church of obnoxious members, but to secure in teaching and conduct strict obedience to the will of Christ by officers and members alike. The system provides at the same time for the greatest degree of true liberty. There is liberty for the lay members who are not subject to clerical rule, as is the case in the Roman Catholic system. The laymen elect their own ministers, and, as elders, govern their own churches with the ministers. There is liberty for the individual churches. These are not to be controlled by a hierarchy as in the system of Rome, but by a local consistory. Even classes and synods do not have higher but only broader powers, being virtually combined or federated consistories. There is liberty for the church in relation to the state. While the Roman Catholics place everything, state included, under the pope as head of the church, and Lutherans and others place the church under the state, the Calvinists fought with their lives for and finally won the liberty of the church from state control. They believe that God has delegated authority to state, church, and other social groups in such a way that each is autonomous in its own sphere.

Morality

There is still one outstanding feature of Calvinistic theology that should be cited. It is the great stress placed on morals, otherwise known as Christian ethics. If you compare Calvinism with Roman Catholicism, or Lutheranism, or Anabaptism, or present-day fundamentalism, Calvinism has by far the greatest stress on morality, as anyone acquainted with the history of these religious groups knows. There is a definite reason for this difference. In the case of the Roman Catholic, the church is at the center of his theology. The important thing, therefore, is that the church member be a good churchman; the rest counts for less. In the case of the Lutheran or fundamentalist, the central fact stressed is some part of man's salvation. The question how to be saved then becomes the important issue. Some fundamentalists today, as the Anabaptists of former years, even claim that the law is no longer in force for the Christian, thereby developing a tendency to an easygoing morality. But when you place God at the center of your system, and everything is made to end in God and his glory, as the Calvinist believes, then even man's salvation becomes a means to a higher end, namely, to win for God a people zealous in good works. It is no wonder that he who places God at the center, as does the Calvinist, should stress a loftier ethic than other Christians do.

There is, however, another reason for the high development of moral life in the Calvinist. It is his consciousness of his total depravity. Other Christian groups are constantly ascribing to man some inherent power. It is a fact that the more you trust in yourself, the less you will trust in God for power. Believing man to be totally depraved, the Calvinist stresses the need of the Holy Spirit as none others do. Calvin was even called the theologian of the Holy Spirit because he stressed as none other the importance of the Holy Spirit for all needs of sanctification. This explains, too, why predestination is stressed. If salvation is only by free grace, of God alone, then God must have decided beforehand to save man, and that means predestination. The effect on moral life of such dependence upon God's power is evident. The man who realizes his helplessness most will depend most upon God, and as a result will draw most upon the riches of God's grace for moral accomplishments (Isa. 57:15; Ps. 51:17).

Such an insistence on a holy life for God accounts for emphasis on the scriptural doctrine of the covenant of grace as you find nowhere else. The covenant of grace stresses especially two facts: Salvation is all by grace; and it demands a well-ordered covenantal life. Observance of covenant obligations rises and falls among Calvinists according as true Calvinism in a given community flourishes or wanes.

Just one more fact about the Calvinistic emphasis on morals must be indicated. The Calvinist believes that when God saves man, he saves the whole man. The whole man must, therefore, be devoted to God's cause—not only when he is at church, but when he is transacting business or engaging in political or social activities of any sort. No sphere of his life may be excluded. Life as a whole must be God-directed; politics, social and industrial relations, domestic relations, education, science and art must all be God-centered. There is no domain of life in which high morals are not essential! God must control the whole of life. Not only individual but social ethics is stressed.

Thus religion attains its highest reach: God in the center of life, salvation alone from God, everything in life for God by power which God himself supplies; there is no loftier ideal of religion conceivable.

6

Common Grace

The study of human life particularly as it is lived among pagans and unbelievers presents a most serious problem. On the one hand statements appear in the Bible which describe pagans and unbelievers as haters of God and of one another, unable and unwilling to do any good, inclined to all wickedness, and totally depraved. On the other hand, a type of life is manifested among these pagans and unbelievers which seems to give the lie to the biblical assessment of their way of life. Calvin calls attention in the following striking manner to this type of life and to the problem it creates:

> If we believe that the Spirit of God is the only Fountain of truth, we shall neither reject nor despise the truth itself, wherever it shall appear unless we wish to insult the Spirit of God. . . . Shall we deny the light of truth to the ancient lawyers, who have delivered such just principles of civil order and polity? Shall we say that the philosophers were blind to their exquisite contemplation and in their scientific description of Nature? Shall we say that those who by the art of logic have taught us to speak in a manner consistent with reason, were destitute of understanding themselves? Shall we accuse these of insanity, who by the study of medicine have been exercising their industry to our advantage? What shall we say of all the mathematics? Shall we esteem them the delirious ravings of madmen? On the contrary, we shall not be able even to read the writings of the ancients on these subjects without great admiration; we shall admire them, because we shall be constrained to acknowledge them to be truly excellent. And shall we esteem anything laudable or excellent, which we do not recognize as proceeding from God?[1]

How Can One Explain the "Excellent" Deeds of the Unregenerate?

How shall we solve the problem of the bad which the Bible ascribes to unregenerate men and those "excellent" deeds performed by these same unregenerate and pagan men? We cannot say of these excellent deeds that they are splendid vices. We cannot call them the products of sin. Sin will not produce such good results. Calvin, after referring to what Paul in Romans 3:10–18 states of the natural wickedness of all men, speaks of the way sin would act in natural man: "There is no furious beast, that would be agitated by such ungovernable rage; there is no river, though ever so rapid and violent, that would overflow its boundaries with such impetuosity."[2]

How then can we account for these laudable deeds found among the pagans and unregenerate? We cannot adopt the view of the Pelagians, who claim that man can still do good like Adam before the fall if he only so desires. The Bible plainly contradicts that view. Nor can we accept the view of the Arminians that God gives to corrupt man enough of prevenient grace that he can of his own nature and choice seek salvation and do the good. Nor can we adopt the view of the Roman Catholics, who hold that for deeds that will merit salvation man needs the supernatural grace of God but that when it concerns doing good on the natural level, man still has native ability to do it, almost as the Pelagians teach. According to Luther and Calvin, man's nature is too depraved to expect any good, in any sphere, arising from that nature itself. Sin, like an ungovernable beast, would destroy and ruin all. If the sinful nature of man had its way, society would be changed into bedlam. The late German concentration camps and the present communist atrocities show what the sinful nature of man will perpetrate if unchecked by common grace.

But how then must we account for those "laudable and excellent" deeds found in the pagan world where the natures are so depraved? Calvin replies:

> In His elect, the Lord heals these maladies. . . . In others, He restrains them, only to prevent their ebullitions so far as He sees to be necessary for the preservation of the universe. Hence some by shame, and some by fear of the laws, are prevented from running into many kinds of pollutions, though they cannot in any

> great degree dissemble their impurity; others, because they think a virtuous life is advantageous, entertain some languid desires after it, others go further, and display more than common excellence, that by their majesty they may confine the vulgar to their duty. Thus God by His providence restrains the perverseness of our nature from breaking out into external acts, but does not purify it within.[3]

The fact is that natural man, however depraved, still has the light of God's revelation in nature (Rom. 1:19–32); man still has a conscience; governments are established "to curb the dissoluteness of men" and to promote "good order and decency" in human society. Men are guided by public opinion, have a sense of the value and advantage of truth, good morals, and the beautiful, though they do not engage in any of these from right motives or with right purposes. Men are restrained from the evildoing to which their sinful nature prompts them by a fear of punishment and are driven on by a sense of reward to do things, contrary to their own sinful nature and choice, which are in outward conformity to the law.

Can These Products of Common Grace Be Called "Good"?

Should we say, then, that unbelievers and pagans do good when they perform deeds that are in outward conformity to the law, when they do these "laudable and excellent" deeds of which Calvin speaks? The answer to that question will depend upon one's definition of "good." In the strict sense of the term anything is good not merely when the outward deed fully conforms to what the law requires, but when the inner disposition of the man who does it is pure. A man can, for example, do a deed which is in outward conformity to the law to his fellowman, just to win his confidence, with the intent to rob and deceive him after he has won his confidence. Such a deed does not meet the requirements of the truly good. The purpose and the disposition must be good as well as the outward act. Good then may be defined as whatever proceeds from a holy heart, is according to the law of God, and is done to his glory. Such deeds which demand a pure disposition and a pure purpose as well as a pure act no pagan or unbeliever can perform. Now proceed a step further. Can a believer do any such good? Again you will have to say, *No*. For not even a deed of a believer ever proceeds from a perfectly pure heart or is performed from perfectly pure motives. The Heidelberg Catechism goes even further in Lord's Day 23, question 60. Here the Christian confesses "that I have grossly transgressed all the commandments of God, and kept none of them and still am inclined to all evil." In that strict sense of the word neither a believer nor an unbeliever can do any good. It is as Jesus said, "None is good, save one; that is God" (Luke 18:19).

But the same Bible which denies good to any save God, at other times does apply the term "good" to the deeds of men. It speaks of Christians as being "zealous in good works." Dorcas was "full of good works" (Acts 9:36). Timothy is told to instruct wealthy Christians to be "rich in good works" (1 Tim. 6:18). Christians, while not perfectly holy, have at least a holy principle in their hearts, and while not perfectly pure in their purposes, have at least a beginning of such purity. No unbeliever's deeds can be motivated by this holy principle of heart. While they may have love for family and love for those who love them, they are never motivated by true love to God or a desire to live for him. Hence their deeds can never be called good, even in the sense that those of the Christian are.

But there is still a third sense in which the Bible speaks of "good" deeds. It is when, whatever may be the motives that prompted one to act, the deed itself at least is in outward conformity to the law of God, although it may have been prompted by selfishness, pride, or fear of punishment. It is in this sense that the works of Jehu, Amaziah, Joash, or other evil men are by the Bible at times called good (cf. 2 Kings 10:29, 30; 12:2; 14:3; Luke 6:33).

This influence of God whereby he through various means restrains vile passions and brings to pass many deeds of outward good by unregenerate men, contrary to the evil principle of sin in their hearts, making them do what their sinful hearts would otherwise not do, is what the Calvinist terms common grace. It is "common" because it is not confined to any unique group as is special grace, but is a grace which is given to all men, though not to all in equal measure. As one believer may have more of special grace than another, so one unbeliever may have more of common grace than another. Thus Calvin compares Camillus, a Roman in whom much common grace was found, with Catiline, in whom there was little of it.[4]

Can These Acts Be the Result of Grace in God?

But can this influence of God, whereby he restrains evil passions and prompts to outward good, truly be called grace? What is grace? The Old Testament word *chen* and the New Testament word *charis*, which are translated by "grace" in our English Bible, have a wide variety of meanings, some of which are irrelevant to our purpose. It is of importance here to note that the word in the Bible may mean (1) an attitude of favor in God to any one; (2) undeserved favor; (3) favor which God works in the hearts of his people whereby he produces faith and conversion; (4) good things which we owe to the favor or grace of God.

The important question for us is this: Does God show any grace, any attitude of favor, and goodwill, any love, to unregenerate, specifically to such that are nonelect or reprobate sinners? We can begin by saying that as reprobate, as sinners, they are never the objects of God's favor, but always of his wrath. God is glorified in the administration of his justice as revealed in the eternal punishment of the wicked. There are many texts in the Bible which express the attitude of hatred of God to the wicked. Nevertheless, that same Bible does express an attitude of favor, even of love of God to nonelect sinners. In Romans 2:4 Paul speaks of the goodness of God to those who will be lost. "Goodness" here means not mere acts of goodness, but an attitude of goodness in God toward those addressed in that verse. This is clear, not only from the meaning of the word, which is "kindness," but also from the synonyms used there—"forbearance" and "long-suffering"—which also express attitudes in God. In Psalm 145:9 we read: "The Lord is good to all, and his tender mercies [an attitude in God] are over all his works." Luke 6:35 instructs us: "Love ye your enemies . . . and ye shall be the children of the Highest, for he is kind unto the unthankful and to the evil."

But how can God love and hate the same persons at the same time? If he hates the wicked, the reprobate, and will punish them for their sins, how can he be said in any sense to love them? According to strict supralapsarian logic, I suppose this is a real problem. For according to this view God, back in eternity, at the outset, decided as his very first decree to glorify himself in two of his attributes, his love and grace toward vessels of honor, the elect, and his punishing justice toward vessels of wrath fitted for destruction, the reprobate. Thereupon, as his second decree, God decided to create these vessels of honor and these vessels of wrath. Note that on this supralapsarian basis the reprobate are already conceived of in the decree of their creation as vessels of wrath. They never were considered objects of love in any sense. The infralapsarian view holds that God first decided to create human beings. As such they were all conceived as objects of his love. Then God decided to permit the fall and in his electing love to save some and to pass by others, the nonelect, and punish them in his wrath for their sins. On this basis it is possible for God to love the nonelect as creatures. A parallel instance would be the case of the righteous father whose heart bleeds for his lost son whose misdeeds demand his expulsion.

Calvin takes this position when he raises the very question here discussed: "Wherefore in a wonderful and divine manner He both hated and loved us at the same time. He hated us, as being different from what He made us; but as our iniquity had not entirely destroyed His work in us, He could at the same time in every one of us hate what we had done, and love what proceeded from Himself."[5] Likewise in his replies to the calumnies made against his view of the secret providence of God, Calvin states in reply to Calumny I:

> Proofs of the love of God towards the whole human race exist innumerable, all of which demonstrate the ingratitude of those who perish or come to perdition. This fact, however, forms no reason whatever, why God should not confine His special or peculiar love to a few, whom He has, in infinite condescension, been pleased to choose out of the rest. When God was pleased to adopt unto Himself the family of Abraham, He thereby most plainly testified that He did not embrace the whole of mankind with an equal love. . . . And in the next place, if God does love His own, it does not the less follow that He has a right to reject as a just Judge those to whom He has in vain shown His love and indulgence throughout their whole lives as the kindest Father.[6]

Thus from the writings of Scripture and from the teachings of Calvin, we learn that God does have an attitude of favor, or grace, to the nonelect, and that this common grace will one day add to their punishment, because it did not lead them to repentance and life for God.

The Benefits of the Calvinistic View Are Far-Reaching

There is great benefit to be derived from this Calvinistic view of common grace. The Anabaptist withdraws from the world, condemning it as a wholly bad manifestation in which nothing but the devil's art operates. The Pelagian and the Roman Catholic seek to maintain that the science, art, and industry of the world are products of good that is still left in natural man. But the Calvinist sees everywhere, in the pagan world and among unbelievers, wherever science, art, and culture are brought to higher levels, the working of God's Holy Spirit, fruits which God has brought to pass in spite of the wickedness of the natural heart of man. The Calvinist thankfully accepts these fruits as products of God's grace and claims them for God's kingdom. Not to withdraw from the world, and on the other hand not to become conformed to the world but to make it his business to use these gifts of God's common grace for the glory of God and for the establishment of his kingdom—that is the duty and the glorious ideal of every good Calvinist.

7

Human Culture

The dictionary defines culture as "any act of cultivating, or the resulting state of being cultivated." It then proceeds to explain what this cultivation means. It signifies "training," any discipline, any refinement which results in improvement, whether of plants, animals, or human beings. One can speak of the culture of plants, of flowers, of bees, and the like. In a more limited sense, however, the word "culture" is restricted to human culture. We then have in mind "any cultivation of human beings which results in their improvement, enlightenment, and discipline acquired by mental and moral training, civilization, refinement in manners and taste."

The word, therefore, has a very broad application. We shall generally employ the term in its more restricted sense as referring to human beings. But even here the word has a variety of meanings. To some the word means little more than the word "polish." When a person begins to work in an office, takes on a veneer of refinement through contact with polite society, learns a few choice phrases, develops a charm of manners, and dresses according to latest fashions, he is by some referred to as a cultured person. By others the term is applied to any person who develops a taste for beauty and art, whether that be of homes or gardens, or paintings, or poetry, or music. Others have a still higher view of culture and use the term in reference to the development of scientific knowledge and the ability which a person acquires of bringing his emotions under control and obeying the law, and of suppressing the lower impulses of his nature. For others culture is equated with love of literature. Any person who has done wide reading of fine books is spoken of as cultured.

The weakness found in all these definitions is that they are fragmentary and call attention to the improvement of only one side of human life. "A thoroughly cultured person is one who is thoroughly matured in every part of his life, so that he is able to fulfill the purpose of his creation."[1] Human culture, then, deals not only with the development of one but all the aspects of human life.

It is important to notice that culture always implies the thought of improvement, not just development. Topsy of *Uncle Tom's Cabin* "jes' growed"; she was not cultured. The great contents of culture, or rather its tools, are, therefore, never merely mechanical and chemical powers of nature, but science, art, technique, ethics, law, the state—always some product of the human mind. It is rather the activity of the human mind applied upon the forces of nature, and bringing creation by the use of these human powers to higher and nobler levels. Culture, in a word, is the fulfilment of the mandate given to man, the king of creation, by his Maker in the garden of Eden: "Keep the garden and dress it." "Have dominion over the earth and subdue it" (cf. Gen. 2). Man was made in the image of God. Just as God is King over the universe and has brought to pass many and noble things in the creation which he made, so he has given to man, his image-bearer, control over nature as his dominion and charged him: "Subdue creation, and bring out the many possibilities in it and in your own nature." Culture is the execution of this divinely imposed mandate. In his cultural task man is to take the raw materials of this universe and subdue them, make them serve his purpose, and bring them to nobler and higher levels, thus bringing out the possibilities which are hidden in nature. When thus developed man is to lay his entire cultural product, the whole of creation, at the feet of him who is King of man and of nature, in whose image and for whom man and all things are created.

Culture in a Sinless World

Had man remained in paradise and had there been no sin, he would still have had the task of culture. In fact "culture" would have been an all-comprehensive term to express what his task would have been in relationship to the world which was placed under him. He would have had to carry out his task in three directions: in relation to nature, to himself, and to the world of humanity. He would have had to control nature and bring out its hidden possibilities. He would have had to develop the image of God in himself. And he, as a member of human society, or organized humanity, would have had to do his share of the common task in developing the rich possibilities of humanity as an organism, which cannot be realized if individuals are working alone.

Let us examine the task of culture as it would have been if there had never been any sin in paradise. By considering culture in a sinless world, we shall perhaps gain a better understanding of what it should ideally be.

The first thing which culture would demand is that man work. For culture means "to develop," to bring out the possibilities for good, to bring to higher levels the things which are in creation and in man himself. This, of course, cannot be done without work. But this work must not bring about mere change, but improvement; otherwise it is not culture. All work that improves, that brings out the possibilities for good, aids in its way the great task of culture.

First to be mentioned and most basic is perhaps the task of farming, otherwise known as agri-*culture*. The farmer subdues the earth and makes it develop its possibilities of crops. In addition to agriculture, there is business, often called barter or trade, in which the products of culture are exchanged, and so brought from one man to another so that man can enjoy in greater measure the products of creation, over which he was made master, than if he were working alone in the world. Next there is industry, manufacture, labor with machinery, a type of work which would also have had its counterpart in a sinless world. Through machinery man is enabled to develop more speedily and efficiently the possibilities which nature has in store for him. All these types of labor are essential for the accomplishment of the cultural mandate assigned to man at his creation.

But there are other types of work in which the activities of the human mind predominate and where, in comparison, there is less of physical labor. When we speak of "culture," we more commonly think of spheres in which there is this greater activity of the human mind. This is but natural. For culture is always the triumph of the human mind over nature, especially over the mechanical and chemical forces of nature. In speaking then of culture we refer especially to the works of science and art. For it is particularly in the realms of science and of art that we see the greatest triumphs of the human mind over nature.

Culture and Science

Let us consider first of the world of science. No one particular kind of science need be examined, but all science, whether it be natural science or the humanities, any kind of science imaginable. In all of them you will find the human mind engaged in examining the works of creation, either the body or the soul, either material things or spiritual things, noting what the nature of each object is, what the idea of it is, how it stands related to other objects, to what class it belongs, and how it forms a part of the world as a whole. The task of science thus reminds us very strongly of the task assigned to Adam when God caused the animals to pass by him. It was Adam's business to discover the nature of each animal, the essential idea of it, and then name it accordingly. This is also exactly the work of science. It does not create the objects but it takes the things God has created, examines them, discovers their underlying ideas and their relationships, and then names them according to its findings. Science continues to do what Adam did at creation, studying things and naming them after their kind. Only of one science is the task somewhat different from the others and that is philosophy. Whereas every other science has a distinct domain in which it performs this task, philosophy, which is called the science of universals, seeks to determine how each of these special sciences fits into a composite whole, into a system of the universe. If philosophy is correct in its findings, it is identical with what the Bible teaches as to the nature of the universe as a whole.

There is another side to the task which science has, however—a more practical one. It is not only the business of science to discover the idea of an object, but also to reveal the value of it for life, to apply that idea to practical use. When the scientist has discovered the essential idea of something, then he must, as toward all the earth, subdue it and make it useful for man. Mere abstract thinking will do no one any good. Its value for life must be shown. The greatest practical usefulness, in which all sciences find their final end and culmination, is that we lay all of those things which we have mastered by science at the feet of the great Master of the universe, God himself.

Culture and Art

There is another sphere in which the mastery of the mind over the forces of nature stands out prominently. It is the world of art. While science has as its task the discovery of the idea of things, art busies itself with giving the idea a corresponding visible or sensuous form. Art deals with symbols. Its task is to picture the idea or image which the artist has conceived of nature in visible form so that we can better appreciate that idea. Not only is it the task of the artist to present nature as it is in its present varying forms, but especially as it ideally should be. The artist presents in his work of art a lofty conception of what something in nature could be when its possibilities are developed. Art is thereby only fulfilling its share of the cultural task, namely, to bring to higher realization the forces resident in nature.

When we speak of art, we at times have in mind what are called the practical or useful arts, any technique or application of special skill to any kind of labor or some cunning workmanship of a master craftsman. But more frequently, when speaking of art, we have in mind the fine arts: architecture, sculpture, painting, music, and poetry.

Let us look at each of these in turn and see how the artist in each case takes some thought of nature, some beautiful idea, and gives it symbolic or visible form. Take the art of architecture. The artist has a conception of some lofty and esthetic thought to which he gives expression in the building he erects, let us say, a cathedral. The cathedrals of Europe are the embodiments of beautiful and lofty conceptions which arose in the minds of talented architects. Whenever a structure fails to express any lofty ideas and consists only of some boards rudely framed, you do not call that structure a work of art. It must be the embodiment of some beautiful thought in sensuous form.

The sculptor does the same thing in his art. He takes not lumber and stone, but a block of marble and begins chiseling it, until he has made it express some living idea—the form of a man or the image of some idea which he has in mind. In the measure that the sculptor's work succeeds in expressing this idea, we call it a work of art. Again, the painter sees a landscape at a distance, or has before him a human being, or draws from imagination some scene of nature as he would have it be, and reproduces that picture on the canvas. In the measure that he succeeds we call the product a work of art. The musician's art does not appeal to the eye, but the ear. But it involves the same underlying process. He has some beautiful thought, some lofty conception, and seeks to give expression to it in sensuous, symbolic form. Insofar as he succeeds impressing this idea upon us through musical tone, in that measure his work is a work of art. The poet does not, like the architect or painter or sculptor, need a tool, unless you call language his tool. Just as the sculptor takes the marble, the painter the brush and canvas, so the poet takes human language and therewith portrays the image of his spirit. His art, therefore, is clearly the most ideological of them all, the most spiritual.

Sin's Effect on Culture

We shall next inquire how sin has affected man's cultural task and how culture stands related to Christianity. Sin has not made man's cultural task unnecessary or superfluous. Sin never makes God's demands unnecessary, nor can it ever thwart God's purposes. We are just as much duty-bound to keep God's laws today as Adam was, even though we cannot keep them because of our enslavement to sin. God's demand, "Subdue the earth, develop it, perform your cultural task," is just as obligatory today as the day God gave it. And God will see to it that the goal of culture is realized and nature's possibilities developed, if not through sinful man, then in some other way.

But sin has made the cultural task doubly difficult. Whereas before sin there was nothing to hinder man in his cultural task, today, the earth, man's dominion, which he must subdue and develop culturally, is cursed. The "thorns and thistles" of which Genesis speaks are an example of countless distorting forces at work in nature today which were not there originally. Instead of all things working harmoniously together and the earth peaceably submitting to man, there are now innumerable conflicts. Nature is distorted. How much more difficult man's task becomes under such circumstances!

Man himself has also changed. No longer has he retained the image of God in that high sense in which he once had it. He has lost the necessary knowledge to understand his cultural task clearly. Instead of continually developing his dominion and leading it to higher levels, he all too often works to its detriment. Instead of being a king who rules over nature, he has in many respects become a slave and lacks the great power he once had to control nature's forces. Not only does each individual man lack the necessary qualifications to carry on successfully his cultural task, but humanity as a whole is impeded. The task which organized society must fulfil in culture by united action is hampered by innumerable conflicts between men, making it hard for them to cooperate. What one builds up, the other breaks down. Mankind, since sin, is working at cross-purposes.

From what has been said one can infer that the full and harmonious cultural development of creation will never come where sin is the controlling factor. Sin always seeks to destroy, never culturally to develop God's creation. Wherever and insofar as sin is dominant in science, or art, or in the moral order of society, sin always disrupts, darkens the mind, and distorts ideals. The consummation of culture will only come when Christ has eliminated the effects of sin. He will free the earth of its curse and restore its normal order. He will renew the image of God in man, and reestablish the harmony between man and his fellow men, between man and nature, and between creation and the will of God. In fact, not only will he restore creation, but he will bring out the possibilities in creation, and develop them to such high levels as we have never dared dream.

If, then, sin tends to break down culture, must we conclude that no culture is possible in heathen lands, where the redemptive work of Christ is not found? Not at all. That would be true if sin were the only force still at work there. For sin would destroy and ruin all. But as we learned in our study of common grace, even in pagan lands God still causes forces to work which counteract the destructive force of sin; and he brings to pass much cultural good despite sin. You need only to look at the high degree of civilization found in several pagan lands of antiquity, notably ancient Greece and Rome, in order to realize that sin has not been able to ruin all. Instead of the wilderness which sin would make of this pagan world, culture is often highly developed. What lofty ideas are at times found in Plato, in Aristotle, in the writings of the ancient dramatists; what admirable works of art, especially of architecture and sculpture, what great logicians and mathematicians are found among them![2]

But no matter how highly their culture was developed, we discover that it failed consistently, especially along two lines. Whether we examine the cultures of Assyria, Babylon, Egypt, Greece, or Rome, we find that they all failed to reach the ideal of true culture, and that in each of these lands the culture contained within itself the germs of its own decay. You realize that they did not reach the ideal of true culture if you study their attitude toward some of the basic facts with which culture must busy itself, namely, man, organized humanity, and nature. What did they think of man? Even the Greeks did not regard all men as fully developed human beings. Woman was not. She was far below man. Nor were all men real men. Slaves were not; only free-born men were considered real men, and even all free men were not real men. Only Greeks were real men. This low idea of man is prevalent in all pagan lands. It has been well said that Jesus Christ first discovered the worth of the individual. He knew the price of a human soul. But even Greeks did not value free-born Greeks, except in what they might mean to the state. How did they estimate humanity, their relations to other men? The Greeks said, "We are Greeks, and all the rest of the world are Barbarians." Other nations spoke in the same disparaging way. They had numerous class distinctions. They never reckoned with the biblical idea that God made of one blood the whole human race. And science, however highly it was developed at times, never grasped man's purpose either for time or for eternity, or the goal God has ordained for nature.

Furthermore, pagan culture had in it the seeds of decay. Even at the times of its highest flower, there was always in that ancient culture the dryrot of sin. Even when the pagans were most abundantly harvesting the fruits of their culture, in science, art, and social life, there existed the cancer of excessive immorality, even in high circles, which spelled defeat. Thus the culture of one land after another crumbled away. Napoleon at St. Helena once is reported, in substance, to have said, "Alexander, Caesar, Charlemagne and myself have founded empires, but upon what did the creation of our genius depend? Upon force. Jesus, alone, founded his empire upon love, and to this very day millions would die for him." This fact is not true of empires alone; it is true of culture in general. Only the culture that is based on Christ, on the Christian foundation, will endure. It seems today as if the culture of Europe is about to decay, drifting away as it does from the ideals, from the power, the grace, the commandments of Jesus Christ. But whatever goes, the church and the kingdom of God, and all that is built upon that immovable Rock, will remain forever.

Christianity and Culture

What has just been stated about the failure of pagan culture shows how needful Christianity is for culture. It would be untruthful to say that culture cannot exist at all outside of Christianity. The fact is there has been culture, at times of a high order, among several of the ancient peoples. But if culture is to accomplish its proper end and is to develop in the right direction with the right ends of creation before it, then it needs the guiding principles of God's special revelation. If culture is to be kept from its own ultimate ruin, as all these pagan nations have experienced, then it needs the moral power of Christianity's Christ.

Is culture itself opposed to Christianity? There are many who affirm that it is and with some show of reason. If you study ancient, medieval, and modern history, you will observe that many in the cultural world of all times have opposed Christianity. Some have done so by polemical criticism and philosophic theories; some by opposing Christians in social, industrial, or political life; others even upon the battlefield, fighting to crush out the Christian religion. It is interesting to note how in scientific circles, or in politics, or anywhere else, men of the world, even those high in society, can differ widely from each other. But the moment Christians become assertive in their religion, either in science or in the formation of a powerful political party, these quarreling men of the world like Herod and Pilate at once become friends and join hands to fight those dangerous Christians. The opposition to the

Christian party in Holland and to the religious parties in Germany are shining examples. Remember that the opposition to Christianity in Nazi Germany did not exist because the Germans had an inadequate culture. In no land was culture so highly developed. The Germans were better educated than we are today. Is not culture then opposed to Christianity?

There are several groups of Christians that assert as much. In fact, not a few fundamentalists today have taken that position. Hence the advice of some in these circles: "Do not seek the advantages of culture, or mingle in learned society. Do not go to college; do not become a physician, or lawyer, or chemist; do not enter into politics or civil service; these are all opposed to your Christian faith. Withdraw from the world, join the society of fellow Christians and save your soul for eternity, but do not concern yourself about the task of culture." They foster a decided separatism between Christianity and the world of culture. The latter is left largely to men of the world, to non-Christian men. The Roman Catholics take a somewhat different stand. They assert that the fruits of culture are good on the natural level as long as these disciplines of the mind are under the control and direction of the church as an institution.

We as Calvinists have in a way the most difficult but also the most biblical position to defend. Wherever culture has developed something worthwhile, whether in Greece, Rome, or among unbelievers anywhere, it is the fruit of what God did among these peoples, contrary to their sinful natures. Sin, if left to itself, will not build up but destroy God's creation. Wherever, then, these fruits of God's common grace appear, it is our duty to make thankful use of them, to the honor of God and to the advancement of his kingdom. Furthermore, as Christians we are obligated to participate in this cultural task of the world. We may not withdraw. For to us today comes the command, "Replenish the earth, and subdue it."

While many in cultured society have frequently adapted the fruits of culture to wrong ends and opposed Christianity, culture itself often helps Christianity. Think of the way in which in the days of the apostles culture aided the spread of the gospel. Think of the way in which the cultural advantages of Paul and his helpers benefited them in meeting the people to whom they brought the gospel; or think of the aid they received in their work from developed roads, the one language which all spoke, or the numerous benefits of the political administration. Note how Calvin insisted that those who studied for the ministry at Geneva should first have a broad cultural training, as he himself had had. When these advantages are spurned, it often works to the detriment of the Christian cause.

Not only is culture often beneficial to Christianity, but Christianity is of the greatest benefit to culture. It is the only means by which culture can ever hope to realize its mission and reach its destined ideal. It is true that many in non-Christian cultural circles have opposed Christianity. But that was due to their evil hearts, not to culture. For culture is just another name for the duty of mankind to develop the raw materials of this world as found in nature and in man himself, to demonstrate the great possibilities inherent in creation, which the Creator has put there, and make them serve the purposes which God has intended they should. One great failing in many cultured unbelievers is that though they discovered the possibilities, the powers, which have offered themselves in the cultural development of the world, they did not understand their proper uses. They used these opportunities for selfish and wicked ends instead of serving God and their fellow men. It is only Christianity which teaches us the purposes for which culture must be used. And it is Christianity which gives to sinful man the regenerative power of the Spirit, which enables and makes man willing to use his powers and his dominion for proper ends.

Best of all, when Christ's redemptive work on earth will be fully realized, out of the ashes of this present world will arise a new universe in which the possibilities for good will be developed a thousandfold. A glorious humanity with perfect culture, so great that eye hath not seen nor ear heard of it, will characterize that earth. When we contemplate that future world with its perfect development, we understand that, far from culture and Christianity being enemies, the triumph of culture will come only through Christianity and Christianity's Christ. All glory to Christ alone, the King also of culture.

It is your duty and mine to labor with all our powers on a Christian basis, for Christian ideals, in every sphere where the Lord calls us so that Christ shall be the recognized King, also in the realm of culture. This is the truly inspiring ideal of culture which we as Calvinists have.

PART

2

Political Ideas of Calvinism

Politics and the Bible

We shall begin our discussion of the Calvinistic principles as they apply to the political world with a brief historical reference. The remark is made at times that Calvinism may be good enough as a theological system but that it has no political program to offer beyond a few general truths concerning the sovereignty of God in all areas of life and the obedience which citizens owe the government. It is claimed that Calvinism has never developed a political system of its own. Or, if it is allowed that it has developed such a system, it is said to consist of mere abstract theories which have never been tried in the political arena to show whether they are workable or not.

Historical Survey of Political Calvinism

To any who might entertain such thoughts, a study of the political history of Calvinism will come as a distinct surprise. Not only has Calvinism developed political principles of its own; but political theories have been framed with these principles as a basis and have been applied in various localities in the modern period of history. Any inquirer who will take the trouble to scan the index of a book on the history of political theories as, for example, *A History of Political Theories* by W. A. Dunning, professor of history and political philosophy at Columbia University (1920), can at once see how large a place in such a work those theories occupy which owe their origin either in whole or in part to Calvinism. An important reason why we hear less today of the Calvinistic views on politics is that our English world in recent years has been unsympathetic to the political views based upon the sovereignty of God and scriptural principles and naturally does not enlarge upon them. If these views are again to become popular, the Calvinists will have to popularize them.

A. M. Fairbairn indicates in substance how important a role Calvin has actually played in political history in the following manner:

> Calvin's chief title to a place in history rests upon his success as a legislator. As a theologian he was a follower, as a legislator he was a pioneer. His system of doctrine was derived, while his political economy broke new ground and based the social edifice on new principles. Certainly he is entitled to the credit of having established a political and legal system on a model of its own, which has profoundly influenced, directly or indirectly, all subsequent democratic institutions.[1]

Jean Jacques Rousseau pays Calvin this high tribute: "Those who consider Calvin only as a theologian fail to recognize the breadth of his genius. The editing of our wise laws, in which he had a large share, does him as much honor as his *Institutes*. Whatever revolution time may bring in our religion, so long as the love of country and liberty is not extinct among us, the memory of this great man will be held in reverence."[2] While we would not attribute to Calvin everything which Rousseau would ascribe to him, it is certain that Calvin was a notable figure in political history and that Calvinism has been highly influential in the political world.

Although it is true that Calvin enunciated political principles which "broke new ground," yet he did not develop a complete Calvinistic theory of the state. This was left for future generations of Calvinists to accomplish. The first to present such a well-developed theory of the state on a Calvinistic basis is perhaps the unknown author of *Vindiciae contra tyrannos,* a political document circulated in France among the French Huguenots during the seventeenth century. The beginnings of a Calvinistic theory of the state are also to be found in a document attributed to Calvin's successor at Geneva, Theodore Beza, entitled *De jure magistratum,* and in

Hotman's *Franco-Gallia,* two works also circulated widely among French Huguenots.

During this general period of history, Buchanan, a celebrated statesman of the reign of Mary Stuart, produced a work, *De jure regni apud Scotos*, in which he developed a political theory solidly rooted in Calvinistic dogma. Although he lacks the fire of the French and Scottish writers, the German Calvinistic scholar Althusius presents the most elaborate systematic treatise on the Calvinistic theory of the state as it was developed in that period of history. In the eighteenth century there is a marked decline of interest in the Calvinistic view of the state. Men like Hugo Grotius and John Locke still used the terminology of the older Calvinists but had drifted far from their political views. Nevertheless, the Calvinists and their theories continued to exert marked influence upon political history, especially in the defense of popular liberties as witnessed in the "Glorious Revolution" of William and Mary (1688) and our own American Revolution (1776).

In the nineteenth century there came a revival of Calvinistic political activity. In England the Anglican statesman William E. Gladstone sought to revive the Christian view of the state largely on a Calvinistic basis. At the same time a similar movement was attempted in Lutheran circles in the days of Bismarck by the able Lutheran philosopher of law, Julius Stahl. Grounding his Christian theory of the state in the sovereignty of God, he developed a political philosophy which in many respects resembled the Calvinistic theory. But his attempt failed to receive the necessary support and was abandoned, although some of his leading principles have remained influential. It is especially in Holland that the Calvinistic theory of the state has been revived through the work of Groen Van Prinsterer, Abraham Kuyper, and Savornin Lohman. In the twentieth century their work has been continued by such men as the late prime minister of Holland, Hendrik Colyn, P. A. Diepenhorst and A. Anema of the Free University of Amsterdam, and several others. Their views also spread to Germany, as W. Kolfhaus informs us in his *Christusbekenntniss und Politik,* published in 1933.

This brief historical reference will give us an inkling of the fact that Calvinism has been of much greater influence upon modern political history than is commonly supposed. Any person who desires to read a survey of these Calvinistic theories is referred to such non-Calvinistic writers as Ernst Troeltsch's *Social Teachings of the Christian Churches and Groups* and Herbert D. Foster's *Political Theories of the Calvinists up to the Time of the Puritan Exodus to America,* in his *Collected Papers,* or to the Calvinistic work of Abraham Kuyper, *Antirevolutionaire Staatkunde* (vol. 1).

We shall present in outline the basic principles of Calvinism as they apply to politics. As we proceed, we shall also call attention to outstanding positions to which these views stand opposed. Perhaps nothing will tend more thoroughly to clarify the Calvinistic views than to point to their opposites. We shall discuss in order the Bible and politics, the state, the government, the citizens, and international relations.

The Bible and Politics

First in order of discussion is the relation of the Bible to politics. The Bible is the Calvinist's rule of faith and practice in everything; therefore it is also his rule in the realm of politics. This is easy to comprehend. According to the Calvinist, God is Sovereign everywhere. Therefore, his Word is also law for the political world. Since the Bible is, as God's Word, his rule of faith and conduct, the Calvinist consults it for guidance in his political activities.

Do not make the mistake of supposing that the Calvinist claims to derive all his ideas from the Bible. This is not the case. As we saw when investigating the place of the Bible in the Calvinistic system, God has two books in which he has revealed himself, the book of nature (i.e., natural objects, history, the lives of men) and the book of Scripture. From nature and from history, therefore, we can learn many facts which the Christian gratefully uses in his political theory. He will trace the political history of empires. He will peruse what students of jurisprudence have thought and taught about the state. But since this book of nature can give us only imperfect views of God and of truth, we need a corrective, and this corrective the Calvinist finds in his Bible. This book of Scripture, besides being the corrective of the book of nature, also contains eternal principles which are to guide the conduct of human society. Therefore, the Bible becomes the book of last appeal and in a special sense the basis for the Calvinist's view on politics.

In adopting the Bible as his foundation in political science, the Calvinist takes a position which is rather unique. Most other systems do not attempt to base their views on the Bible. As their authority in affairs of state they will appeal, not to the Bible, but to some such ground as the will of the masses, or the individual sentiment of justice, or natural rights; or they will make of the state an autonomous body, which can decide what it will—always some human ground. This does not imply that adherents of such political systems will always object to your having religious views. Some who are atheists will object to it as the Soviet government is doing. Others are quite willing to allow religious opinions, but they maintain that these religious views should be private matters and should not be injected into politics. Others will go even further and allow religion to color certain political activities, such as the opening of political gatherings with prayer or occasional reference to God in speeches. But when it comes to the drafting of political views, they maintain that the Bible may not be the criterion. In politics, human opinions and human theories must decide. The Calvinist goes back to God. The will of God is determinative for the views which he must hold concerning the state.

How are we to understand the statement that the Bible is the Calvinist's foundation in politics? Does the Calvinist expect the Bible to provide him with a political platform? It would be folly to expect such a thing. A political party in the United States changes its platform every four years. Despite such frequent changes it is a difficult matter to draft a platform which will satisfy all sections of the country. How then could anyone reasonably expect the Bible to supply a platform which would hold good for all ages and all classes? In fact, the Bible does not even offer us any organized political system which we can use. It does not even offer us a unified theological system. There is a more or less developed political plan presented in the Bible, the so-called Mosaic theocracy, that civil-ceremonial system found in the first five books of the Bible. But that system, according to the very words of Calvin, was made for other times and other conditions and does not hold good for today. In fact, the Calvinist does not believe that there is one hard and fast system of government which the Bible advocates. The Bible does not declare that the government must be a monarchy, or an aristocracy, or a democracy. The Bible offers eternal principles which should underlie and control all political systems. These principles never grow old, but like all principles they are eternal, changeless, and pertinent for all times and all conditions. When once one has mastered these principles, then one can build systems and construct platforms to meet existing conditions, and can critically analyze them to judge whether or not they are sound.

Where in the Bible are these principles to be found? Some think these principles are only to be found in isolated texts of the Bible. And if they are not very successful in finding suitable texts, they soon come to the conclusion that the Bible must not have much to say about politics. The Calvinist believes that the biblical basis for his political or his theological or his social views is not to be found in mere isolated texts. He rather discovers these principles in the rule of faith that runs through the whole of Scripture and manifests itself in a variety of ways, also at times in special texts, such as, "Let every soul be subject unto the higher powers," or "By me kings reign" (Rom. 13:1; Prov. 8:15). But these principles are not at all confined to such special texts.

These principles deal not only with such very general matters like the sovereignty of God and the duty of obedience to governments, but also with many other political problems, such as the relation of the individual to the group, the relation of churches and other organizations in society to the state, the limits of governmental power, and the rights of individuals. Calvin in developing his political views made much of such biblical principles as justice, equity, and the well being of the people.

The Calvinist insists that the principles of God's Word are valid not only for himself but for all citizens. Since God is to be owned as Sovereign by everyone, whether he so wishes or not, so also the Bible should be the determining rule for all. But especially for himself, the Christian, according to the Calvinist, must in politics live by these principles. He declares that not only with his soul for eternity, but as well in matters that concern his body in time, he belongs to his faithful Savior Jesus Christ. Him, therefore, he must obey in all walks of life.

The great value of adopting the Bible as his unconditional, positive rule of faith and life, also for political matters, will become increasingly clear as we study the various aspects of Calvinistic political theory.

9

The Origin and Function of the State

The state may be defined as a political community which resides in a given territory, is organized under a distinct government, and is recognized by the people as supreme. The state differs from a mere society in that it implies a government. In addition to having a government, the society must dwell in a definite territory of its own. A wandering band of nomads, for example, gypsies, even though they may have a king of their own, is not a state. States always have their own physical domain.

The Origin of the State

How do states originate? We can learn much about the reason why they exist by asking ourselves that question. It is a plain historical fact that all states have not originated in exactly the same way. The United States has arisen in one way, England in another, and Germany, France, Holland in still other ways. Perhaps no two states have originated in exactly the same manner. But, to say that all states have had a somewhat different origin does not solve the problem. The question still needs to be answered: Why do all societies of people, the one group after one pattern, another in a somewhat different way, organize themselves into states with rulers and laws by which they are governed?

Various explanations have been suggested. Some claim that

the formation of states is due to nothing more than an old custom. In the evolution of the race the state arose as a mere tribal custom or tradition. If only inveterate custom is at the basis of the state, one can readily perceive its meagre moral basis. Any group that would so desire might then have the right to overthrow the authority of the state as long as it had the brute power necessary. Others claim that the rise of the state is due to some agreement made by men in primitive times. According to some of these theorists, originally every man was a wolf to every other man. To protect themselves against each other, men agreed to form a state. Others hold that the formation of the state was due to the development of a more complex society. Originally, so they argue, every man was his own master and could do as he pleased. But as society became more intricate, men could not accomplish the needs of more involved life unless they entered upon a contract in which they agreed to work for these common ends. This social contract necessitated the formation of states with governments and laws, since some men then needed to be masters over other men to meet the needs of organized society. These are a few samples of how, according to opinions commonly held, states arose. There is in the origin of states, according to these opinions, nothing providential, not even an inherent natural cause but merely a custom, or a mutual agreement, which might have been neglected, except for some practical benefit which men sought.

According to the Calvinist, the state is a natural formation. It arises from a social impulse, a *Sozial-trek,* placed in man by God. In holding to this view, the Calvinist is not alone. Already the heathen philosopher Aristotle recognized that there is not only an individual but a social strain in man as well. Some speak of a "gregarious instinct" in man which makes men group together in families, tribes, and clans. The Calvinist believes that this "gregarious instinct" is implanted in man by the One who created him.

However, this cohesive social instinct alone cannot account for the origin of the state, since the state is more than a mere society. It is a society plus a government under which it is organized for definite purposes. The moment a group living in an independent territory band themselves together to promote the general welfare of the group, to secure common ends, they need the machinery of government, rulers, laws, courts of justice, and police, armies and navies to enforce these laws. This state formation, in which the members of human society appoint governments for the promotion of the common interests and the general welfare of the group, and for the administration of justice, is also a providential arrangement of God for man.

If the world had not fallen into sin, there would still have been, in a sense, a state, namely, a society of men under a government recognized by the people as supreme. In fact, there would have been a perfect state, the kingdom of God. In this state some men would have held positions of rulership over other men. Evidence of this can be adduced from the fact that in the sinless world of heaven, in addition to the archangel Michael, some of the angels called "thrones, dominions, principalities and powers" are rulers over other angels. And in the new earth wherein dwelleth righteousness, some men will have positions of rulership over other men. The twelve apostles of the Lamb will be judges, ruling the twelve tribes of Israel. And those who will have gained ten pounds will "have authority over ten cities" (Luke 19:12–27).

The Function of the State in a Sinless World

The question may be asked what the governmental task of these rulers in a sinless world will be. There will be no need to make and enforce laws, since all will know and do what is right. The answer lies in the cultural task with which God has entrusted man at his creation, as explained more fully in the previous chapter on culture. Each man in a sinless world would have as his individual obligation the development of the image of God in himself and the performance of his cultural task insofar as it concerned his own personal interests. Besides these individual tasks, each family would have its group activities to perform. In the nature of the case these individual and family activities would expand as human society would expand. But humanity as a whole would also have a united task to perform, corresponding to the cultural task which the organism as a whole would have to accomplish. The common activities, implied in the united work of the group as a whole, would require that some men act for the group in positions of leadership. The reason for this would be that the individual wills, though perfect, must be united in these leaders in oneness of will and purpose. The direction of the group affairs by these leaders of the social unit would vest them with a ruler's authority. At the head of this vast empire—for it would be organically one—would stand Adam, the physical and federal head of the human race. But there would be no need of statutory laws, or courts of justice, or police, or armies, or navies, since perfect peace and harmony would prevail. This part of a government's task would, therefore, not exist.

The Function of the State in a World of Sin

Since the entrance of sin into the world, the type of government had to be modified to meet the changed conditions. The government now needs authority to enact laws against the transgressor, courts of justice to explain and decide in given cases of law, and a police force to make effectual the statutes. This authority has been entrusted to governments by God since the fall, as we learn from the Bible in Romans 13:1–4, where we read that the government has been given the power of the sword and the right to labor for the punishment of evildoers and for the praise of them that do well.

Do not suppose, however, that the perfect kingdom of God in which all men will live in perfect harmony and cooperation in the common cultural task of society, which has been lost by sin, is either continued in or will be brought to pass by governments as we now have them. History proves that the kingdom of God and ideal social conditions can never come about through natural development, either by governments or any other natural way. This great ideal, the kingdom of God, that perfect state, will alone be realized by Jesus Christ, and not by natural means but by supernatural grace. That kingdom he has already planted in this world. It is begun in regeneration, continued in sanctification, and consists in this present dispensation in spiritual realities only; but it will one day become both spiritual and material when, as a result of his redemption, out of the ashes of this old world will arise a new earth wherein dwelleth righteousness. And over this kingdom of God, which is the continuation of that royal power over the kingdom of

God at creation, Christ, the last Adam, and not the state's authorities, has been placed. Furthermore, this task of Christ belongs in the realm of special grace and lies in the domain of the church, not of the state.

What then is the business of the state, if it is not the continuation of the kingdom of God at the beginning of human history? The answer is, as indicated in Romans 13 and suggested in a former paragraph, that the government is a mechanical device, ordained by God in his common grace for the punishment of evildoers and for the praise of them that do good. This "good" is not to be limited to such human tasks as each individual must himself perform, but refers as well to his part in the common task of the group. The fact that man cannot realize the ideals of creation does not exonerate him from his responsibility, either as an individual or in the tasks which mankind unitedly must perform. Men must still as states unite for these common ends. Speaking of the function of governments, Calvin warns against two dangers. First, he warns against the danger of identifying the state with the kingdom of God; second, against supposing that these two have nothing to do with each other. Says Calvin, "But as we have just suggested that this kind of government is distinct from that spiritual and internal reign of Christ, so it ought to be known that they are in no respect at variance with each other."[1] He then proceeds to ascribe to the government a wide range of duties: (1) to support the church; (2) "to regulate our lives in a manner requisite for the society of men"; and (3) to administer civil justice. Elsewhere he speaks of the duty of the government to provide for the general welfare of society. And Abraham Kuyper, who stresses very emphatically the duty of the government as a measure of God's common grace in the administration of justice, also asserts that the government has the duty to effect such ends as demand the cooperation of all, as promoting the general welfare and preserving unity amidst diversity.[2]

From the preceding statements it may be inferred that the authority of the state is not absolute, covering the whole of life, but definitely limited. It would be so even in a sinless world, for the individual and the family and whatever spheres would naturally have developed out of these private spheres, would have had their own special cultural duties to perform independently of the state. But in a sinful world these spheres which are independent of the state are even more numerous. Some, like the church, owe their existence entirely, and some, like schools of science, owe their existence partially to God's grace as it existed after the fall. These groups are rooted in a principle of their own and have their own task to perform independent of the state and do not concern the general welfare or task of the state. The state then is limited in its social task to the promotion of such cultural interests as concern the group as a whole, the public welfare, of what has been called the *bonum commune naturale* (the natural, common good), in distinction from all these private spheres of individuals, families, church, and society. In addition to this cultural task, the state after sin is also entrusted with administration of justice among the members of society, toward each other, and to the state as a whole.

10

The Best Form of State

In the last chapter we indicated the main functions of the state according to the Calvinistic conception. In the present chapter we shall demonstrate which type of state the Calvinist would consider ideal—the God-ordained one—to accomplish these functions.

The State in a Sinless World and in Today's World

If the world had remained sinless, there could be no uncertainty as to the character of the ideal state. It would be one world-state, a world empire, the kingdom of God. The type of government would be monarchical with Adam at the head of this empire, with several lesser authorities under him. And in the new earth there will once more be a world empire under the last Adam, Christ, as King, in which there will be the proper subordinate officers also.

But there will never be a God-ordained world empire in this sinful world. In fact, just to curb the dissoluteness of men, God divided the peoples of the earth into several nations and languages at the tower of Babel. Various attempts, however, have been made to erect world empires, not upon a Christian basis, seeking to reestablish a kingdom of God (though this has been repeatedly tried on a small scale), but on a basis of force. The Antichrist will again seek to establish a world empire on the basis of force. But his empire will be destroyed by Christ. It may be said that Calvin favored states which are not overly large in order to offset the danger inherent in an excessive concentration of power in one government.

Calvinism, therefore, does not favor the existence of one state or world empire in a sinful world. Neither does it favor any one type of government, be it monarchy, aristocracy, democracy, or any other one type. It might be supposed that Calvinism would favor the reintroduction of the Mosaic theocracy into the modern world. In fact, Calvin is often represented as if he had that desire at Geneva. This claim is made in the face of the fact that Calvin repeatedly asserted that the Mosaic theocracy was never intended for anything but the Israelitish nation. Several of its laws are designed to fit conditions other than those of the present day. Just as in God's providence the one world empire has been divided since sin into several states, so also the authority of governments has been divided. God can rule not only by one (monarchy), but as well by a few (aristocracy), or by several, or even all (democracy). In fact, not only can God so rule, but he actually does. As the Bible informs us: "There is no power but of God, the powers that be are ordained of God" (Rom 13:1). Since the Bible declares that God rules through various types of government today, the question of the mode of government men should have in any given instance resolves itself into a practical one; namely, which kind will operate best for the purposes of government?

The answer to this question will not be the same in all cases. In some countries one system of government will operate best, in others another type. In the United States the democratic pattern works best. But in some other lands, where the moral and cultural levels are not so high, as in the South American republics, the democratic form is constantly suffering from revolutions. And in a country like China it is questionable whether a real democracy will work at all. Likewise, at one period in a nation's history the democratic form of government may succeed, but when morals decline and men disregard law and authority, a dictatorship or monarchy may become necessary to compel obedience which was not willingly rendered and to bring order out of chaos.

In the abstract there are arguments in favor of and against each form of government. In a monarchy the power is placed in the hands of one person. This makes for unity and efficiency of administration. But the dark side is that the bearer of that authority may easily misuse his power for the benefit of his favorites or of himself. In a democracy the power rests in the hands of the people. This is a great safeguard against oppression, fosters the interest of all in political affairs, and creates a sense of responsibility. But the defects are that action is slow and that there is danger of party politics being dominant. In an aristocracy, again, the noblest spirits are supposed to rule. But the danger here is that the interests of the few may predominate, that class distinctions and class hatreds may be engendered. The best guarantee of the workability of a government lies not in its form (monarchy, aristocracy, or democracy) but in the moral and spiritual fiber of the people. With good people almost any kind of government will work. With absolutely depraved people no type will work. Perhaps a monarchy will succeed best where force is needed and a more democratic type where the moral and cultural levels are highest. One thing is certain: moral and spiritual background is essential to successful government, and upon this the Calvinist, with his fundamental principle of the sovereignty of God and human responsibility, strenuously insists.

It is worthy of note that Calvin in the *Institutes* favored either an aristocratic type of government or a mixture of aristocracy and democracy for the countries of Europe. His reason was that kings rarely so rule that their will is not at variance with justice and rectitude. Besides, Calvin argued, kings are not endowed with the wisdom and penetration necessary to discover consistently what is best. In his later works, the commentaries published between 1550 and 1560, notably in *Deuteronomy* and *Samuel,* Calvin's utterances are still more strongly in favor of the democratic type of government.

The State and Christianity

Must the state be a Christian state? This is a highly important question over which many sharp conflicts have arisen. The question is not to be answered with a simple "yes" or "no." It depends upon what is meant by the term "Christian." There is a very legitimate sense in which it is true that the state is not a Christian institution at all. The state is an institution of God's common grace in this world by means of which God in his providence checks sin and promotes a moral world order. This institution, however, exists not only where Christianity is found, but long before and outside the boundaries of Christianity, among Mohammedans, Buddhists, Zoroastrians, the ancient Greeks and Romans, people who have not been influenced by the principles of Christianity. And yet, so the Bible informs us, all these governments were instituted by God. The state as an institution is, therefore, not a distinctly Christian formation.

There is a second sense in which the term "Christian" has been applied to states. Whenever a state is permeated with a Christian spirit and applies Christian principles in the administration of civic affairs, it is called "Christian." If that is what is meant by a Christian state, then all states should be Christian, according to the conscience of the Calvinist, even though many states are not Christian. If God is the one great Sovereign of the universe, it is a self-evident fact that his Word should be law to the ends of the earth. The state may never be an atheistic state, denying God's law or his sovereignty, as the Soviet Union has attempted. Nor may it be a neutral state, as adherents of liberalism in politics have desired. If God is Ruler, no man may ever insist that religion be merely a private matter divorced from any sphere of society, political or otherwise. God must rule everywhere! The state must bow to his ordinances just as well as the church or any private individual. The Calvinist, whose fundamental principle maintains that God shall be Sovereign in all domains of life, is very insistent on having God recognized in the political realm also.

It is, indeed, true that the state has been given a separate domain by God. It is not called to do the work of the church. It is not the God-ordained institution for the propagation of religion. Nevertheless, for matters which relate to its own domain as state, it is as bound to the Word of God as the church or the individual. A state is Christian in this sense when, with God's Word as its guide, its government maintains respect for authority, punishes evil according to divine ordinances, does not seek to disregard the guilt and responsibility of government officials or of its citizens, maintains the sanctity of marriage and the human family, guards the Sabbath, promotes philanthropy, honors the church and its mission in this world, and in similar ways reveals that it is permeated with the Christian spirit insofar as this relates to its own sphere of government.[1]

There is still a third way in which the term "Christian" might be understood as relating to the state; namely, in this sense, that Christ is recognized as the Ruler of the state just as he is of the church, so that all government officials are adjudged to be subject to his command. Various groups in the Christian church have maintained this position, as the Arminians, the Erastians, and the Roman Catholics. These all held to the theory that Christ is head of the state as well as of the church, though they were led to diverse conclusions in the application of this principle.

These groups could with some show of reason appeal to the Bible for proof that Christ was made head of the state. Let us cite just a few Scripture texts which refer to Christ's universal authority. In the Fourth Gospel, John says (John 3:35), "The Father loveth the Son, and hath given *all things* into his hand." In John 17:2 we read, "As thou hast given him power over all flesh." It is especially worthy of note that, according to Matthew 28:16–20, Christ declared, just before he ascended to heaven and sat at God's right hand: "All power is given unto me in heaven and in earth. Go ye, therefore, and disciple all nations . . . teaching them to observe all things whatsoever I have commanded you." If Christ has been given all authority in heaven and on earth, should not the state as well as the church recognize Christ as its King and even promote as part of the state's business the true church of Christ?

The Arminians at the time of the Synod of Dordt in 1618 defended this view. We usually think of the Arminians as differing from the Calvinists only on the doctrinal issue of the question of election and free will as it was discussed at that synod. But an equally burning question for that synod was whether and how far the civil government had authority over the church. The Arminians, led by such illustrious men as Oldenbarneveld and Hugo Grotius, maintained that though the church had the right to formulate its doctrinal views, the state was to have control over the government of the church.[2] They defended this view with an appeal to Scripture references such as those cited above. Christ was the head of the state as well as of the church. Therefore, according to them, the government which was given the power to rule should also rule the church, doctrinal matters being left to the church officials to decide.

Others in the Christian church went a step further than the

Arminians, notably in England and in Germany. The government should decide not only in the governmental affairs of the church, but in doctrinal matters as well. They resurrected a view formerly promoted by the ancient Romans; namely, that the civic ruler was not only the chief ruler over everything in the state, but also the chief high priest in the religion of the state, the so-called *pontifex maximus*.

When the Roman government became nominally Christian in the fourth century, Constantine continued this Roman custom, taking over the headship of the church with the mere change in title from *pontifex maximus* to *episcopus universalis*, universal bishop. The Christian rulers after him sought to maintain an identical position in the church, with an appeal to the same set of Scripture texts. Since Christ had authority over all flesh, they, representing his authority on earth, should be head of both branches into which society was divided in their day, the state and the church. Some present-day rulers in totalitarian states are assuming the right to be supreme heads of the church with no attempt to defend their action scripturally.

The Roman Catholics started from exactly the same premise—the authority of Christ over all the earth—but arrived at the very opposite conclusion from the one defended by the Christian emperors. The ruler of the state was not simultaneously to be the head of the church, but the ruler of the church, the pope, was supposed to govern the state. Christ had all authority in heaven and on earth. The pope was the vicar of Christ on earth. Therefore, the pope is supreme ruler on earth over both church and state. In token of this supposed authority the pope, even today, wears the papal tiara, a triple crown, which is designed to indicate that he is head over three realms: the church, the state, and purgatory. When the power of the state began to wane in the Middle Ages and that of the church increased, this theory was brought to triumph by the popes, especially by Gregory VII (A.D. 1075).

What is the error in all these theories? The error lies in a faulty exegesis of the relevant Scripture passages. The Bible indeed does state that Christ the Mediator has been given authority over all flesh, and all power in heaven and on earth. However, it does not thereby mean to suggest that Christ has authority over the state as its Ruler, as he is of the church. Christ is directly appointed Ruler over the church and over the kingdom of God. This rulership is given him as a reward for his mediatorial work. But this rulership lies in the sphere of special grace. As far as his redemptive work spreads its wings, he is Ruler and governs by his Word and by his Spirit. As Christ stated: "My kingdom is not of this world" (John 18:36).

But the state, which is, as we know it today, a creation of God's common grace, does not come under the rulership of Christ as redeeming Mediator. A clue as to how he nevertheless can be said to have authority over all flesh is given us in Ephesians 1:22, where it is stated that God hath put all things under Christ's feet, "and gave him to be the head over all things to the church." This phrase, "to the church," suggests a very definite limitation of Christ's authority over all things as Redeemer. As Ruler over the church and the kingdom of God, Christ must protect it and direct its destiny through a hostile world. To enable him to do this, he as the Redeemer must be given authority to control all things so that, no matter what these forces may choose to do, Christ has the authority and power from God to control their actions, restrain any possible evil, and direct all things for the benefit of his church and kingdom. Even Satan is subjected to this jurisdiction of Christ so that not even the gates of hell can prevail against the church. This authority, manifestly, is something very distinct from that asserted in the claim that Christ as Redeemer is administrative Ruler over the state as he is over the church. The state, which is a creation of God's common grace, not of special grace, is, to be sure, subject to the rule of the Triune God as Creator and, therefore, subject to the Word of God as a rule of life. But it is not subject to Christ as the Mediator of redemption. In this last sense, therefore, the state cannot properly be designated as Christian.[3]

At the close of our discussion of the Calvinistic view of the state, it is well to keep the following summary of facts before us. The state was originally instituted by God to care for those cultural interests which the people unitedly were to dispatch in distinction from such tasks as belonged to individuals, the family, and whatever spheres might develop from these private interests. This kingdom of God is not continued in the contemporary state, but in the supernatural kingdom planted by Christ on this earth by special grace, and it will be consummated on this earth after the Judgment Day. The state of today is a mechanical device, an instrument of God's common grace which should not work at variance with God's kingdom but favor its promotion through the church. Mankind after the fall still has its cultural duties to perform. Some of these tasks are the particular interest of the individual, the family, the church, or science. It is not the business of the state to discharge these duties. But there are also tasks which are to be performed by the entire group. The task of the government is this general task, sometimes spoken of as the *bonum commune naturale* (the natural common good). In addition to this task the state has the duty, since the entrance of sin into the world, to administer justice among the members of human society toward each other and toward the group as a whole. In the performance of this task it is to be guided by God's Word and is subject to the sovereignty of the Triune God, though not to the Mediator Christ, since the domain of the state is not under special grace but under common grace.

11

The Form of Government

Having read the title of this chapter, some might involuntarily be inclined to look for a hard and fast system of government which can be labeled the Calvinistic political system. In vain will we look for any such thing. It is indeed true that Calvinism is a system of truth, a philosophy of life, a world- and lifeview with a set of pertinent political principles. But Calvinism makes no claim to mechanical uniformity. As to form, it is not something static, fixed once for all, incapable of development or modification to meet changing conditions. It is rather like an organism of truth, full of life and the power of adaptation.

Even in its formation of churches, Calvinism does not advocate a mechanical uniformity. All true Calvinistic churches do reveal a unity of principle, yet how much variation we find in their more than thirty confessions and in their historic church formations! How different the churches of Reformed persuasion in Holland are from those in Scotland, and these again from the Calvinistic churches in England or America; how different the Westminster Confession from the Heidelberg Catechism or these from the Belgic Confession! The same is true of the Calvinistic state formation. While there is a unity of principle apparent in them all, yet in the history of Calvinistic states from Calvin's time down to the present, there has been a constant development along Calvinistic lines to meet ever-changing conditions.

Likewise there has been a difference in the application of the political principles of Calvinism in the same era of history, as the needs of the various countries demanded. How different, for example, the development was in the city-state of Geneva than in Scotland or in America. A thoroughly Calvinistic government may be a limited monarchy or it may be a republic, and it may have a variety of laws and functionaries without losing any of its particular Calvinistic traits. This power of adaptation to ever-changing conditions without loss of distinctiveness is one of the prime virtues of the Calvinistic pattern. This keeps it contemporary.

Only the distinguishing traits, since these explain the Calvinistic attitude toward the government, will, therefore, be presented here. The first and all-important characteristic, the basic principle of Calvinism which meets us wherever there is genuine political Calvinism, is the recognition of the sovereignty of God and the supreme authority of the Word of God in its application to political conditions. It is said of Calvin that in the history of political schemes he broke virtually new ground when he erected his political edifice on biblical principles. Wherever you find genuine Calvinism operating in any political field, there you find the same insistence upon the sovereignty of God and obedience to the Word of God as it concerns matters of state.

Advantage for Authority

By adopting this fundamental position, Calvinism placed itself very definitely on the side of law and order as against rugged individualism and all disregard of the rights of others or the rights of the community. It made for highly stable governments. It strenuously demanded respect for authority and obedience of citizens to the government. In fact, the very highest of motives was advanced for such respect for authority and obedience, namely, that God demanded it. And it obviated all excuse for subjectivism and selfish individualism by adopting an objective and perfect regulative standard for man's conduct in political affairs, namely, the Bible as the Word of God.

Advantage for Popular Liberty

This leads us to the consideration of the question of whether Calvinism, which is admittedly a strong force for law and order and for obedience of the citizens to the state, makes adequate provision for the defense of the rights and liberties of citizens against possible tyrannies of governments. Does it present any safeguards against state absolutism and the destruction of all rights of the people? There is, of course, a constant struggle between authority and liberty, an ever-present danger that the one will suffer at the expense of the other. What did Calvinism propose as a safeguard? The answer to this important question is written large on the pages of Calvinistic history. Calvinism has risen to the defense of popular rights and liberties by various provisions. Only insofar as these affect the form of government which Calvinism favors, can we note them in this chapter. We would list especially the following five safeguards characteristic of Calvinistic governmental ideals.

There is, first of all, its opposition to any one world-state in this sinful world or even to any overly large states. It favors smaller states in order, as Calvin expresses it, to offset the danger of dictatorial power in the hands of a few men. While it does favor the cooperation of the family of nations for the promotion of peace and the regulation of mutual rights of nations, it never favored the unification of all into one or a few nations. Just as God at the tower of Babel broke up an attempted world empire to curb the dissoluteness of men, so the Calvinists were against excessively large states for the same reason.

Nor does Calvinism favor the concentration of power within any one single nation, large or small, in the hands of one or a few men. Its historic opposition to absolute monarchies and aristocracies and its favor of republican forms of government are well known. It feared monarchs and dictators. To offset the danger of oppression arising from such sources, it sought a safeguard in the constitutional form of government and in the control of governmental actions by the citizenry. The Calvinists were not satisfied with charters, which were only grants of privileges to the people by ruling sovereigns; but the Calvinists demanded well-defined constitutions in which the legal rights of the people were definitely stipulated. And the members of parliament or congress were regarded as the people's representatives, appointed for the defense of their rights against all autocratic usurpation of power or illegal exercise of authority by the king and other government officials. More emphatically still, the people had the right to voice their approval or disapproval of governmental actions by vote or by the expression of public opinion.

This promotion of constitutional government the Calvinist defended by an appeal to his religion. The Bible—his guide book—taught him that even such monarchs as were directly appointed and anointed by God, as Saul and David, were not inducted into office without the voice of the people. And when men like Jeroboam and the wicked kings of Israel who followed him led Israel to the worship of the golden calves, Israel was taken to task for not rebelling against such leadership. If then the people had the right of control and the duty to defend God's law and justice against the autocracy of kings in Israel—thus the Calvinist argued—why should the same not be true in any nation?

Added to this was the fact that in the most sacred institution on earth, the church, there might be no ignoring of the people's rights by those in power. The Roman Catholic Church gave the people no voice in the government of the church, but placed it in the hands of the priesthood, who in turn were all subject to the pope, thus resulting in a purely monarchial system of church government. Even the Lutherans denied the laity any governing power in the church.

The Calvinists, on the other hand, lodged the governing power in the hands of the laity as elders. And when the elders were placed in authority, the members of the church were given the right of control over the acts of the consistory, as partakers of Christ's kingly anointing. If then in the most sacred institution on earth, the church, the government of which the Calvinist patterned after the Bible, the people were given governmental authority and lay members even had the right of control—thus the Calvinist argued—why not in political institutions as well? For the Calvinist, the government of the church became in practice a model for state formation.

Another safeguard against concentration of power in the hands of a few is found in the division of government into its three branches—the legislative, the executive, and the judicial—without the subordination of any one of them to the other. This division of government into three coequal branches is a trait characteristic not only of the Calvinist system. Aristotle already recognized the value of dividing the functions of government and keeping them on an equal footing to guard against autocracy of rulers. With respect to the U.S. government Woodrow Wilson remarks in his book, *The State,* "With a fine insight into the real character of the government which they were constructing, the Convention provided that its judiciary should be placed, not under the President or the houses, but alongside of them, upon a footing of perfect equality with them."[1] This view of government has been jeopardized today, notably in Spain and the Soviet Union where the legislative and judicial bodies are so subordinated to the executive branch of government as to be little more than figureheads. The early Calvinists of the United States, as well as of other lands, were eager to keep these branches separate and of equal importance to offset the possible danger of autocracy and to protect the popular liberties.

A very important safeguard of popular rights and liberties is to be found in the Calvinistic theory of the sovereignty of each distinct social body in its own sphere, as for example, the home, the school, the church, and commercial and other social organizations. Because each of these organizations is rooted in a principle of its own, has received its own God-given task, and does not owe its rise or existence to the state, the Calvinist maintains that each of these organizations is sovereign whenever it is engaged in matters which relate strictly to its own sphere. One can readily see how this view tends to restrict state interference in each of these provinces to definite limits. Only when certain conditions arise which jeopardize the well-being of the state or of others in society is state interference in the home or school or similar units warranted.

There is still another political view of the Calvinists which has important bearing upon the question of the rights and liberties of the citizens toward the central government. It is implied in the terms "decentralization" and "local autonomy." In ecclesiastical life the Roman Catholics and the Calvinists represent two opposing forms of church government. In the Roman Catholic Church all is governed by the central power, the pope. All churches are branches organized and controlled by this central government, lodging all power in the central authority at the expense of local autonomy. The Calvinists begin with the local church as a complete church. This body then delegates some of its power to the classis or presbytery, and these to the synod or the general assembly. The power of the central government, in this case, comprises as much as the constituent bodies have delegated to it, but the rest of the power is retained by themselves.

Essentially these same two forms of government are found in different states: the former in France, where every village and hamlet is, in the last analysis, ruled by the central governing body in Paris; the opposite system, in the United States. While in France there exists a national bureaucratic government, and all local bodies and the individual citizen are kept in tutelage to the central control, in the United States the separate states are not administrative divisions but constituent members of the federal union. The states in their own spheres are subordinate to the federal union, not "in the sense of being subject to be commanded by it, but only in being less than national in scope."[2] The same fact is essentially true in the individual states and in all county, township, and local city governments. Though in each state there exists a single plan of statutory laws for the whole state, yet the executive power is put into the hands of the local authorities. "Local administration is the administration of the state."[3]

The U.S. system of government is, in this respect, in agreement with historic Calvinism and provides the greater amount of liberty to the citizen. Hendrik Colyn, the former Calvinistic prime minister of Holland, made a strong plea for local autonomy and decentralization, with preservation of proper and sufficient power for the central government for the execution of its own national affairs. He rejected the idea that the present complex condition of society demands that this local autonomy be taken away.

Although Colyn admitted that in contemporary society all parts of the state are being brought into closer contact and interrelationship, he maintained that the reason why, in former days, groups had local self-government, was not the difficulties which central governments might have in controlling all sections, but rather the demand for local self-government.

The Anti-Revolutionary party of Holland, of which Colyn was leader, has given expression to this Calvinistic principle of local autonomy in the tenth article of its program of principles as follows: "The Anti-Revolutionary Party desires that the territorial and local autonomy, insofar as this does not conflict with the demands of the unity of the State or leave the rights of individuals unprotected, be allowed by decentralization to receive its due rights."

We have mentioned in the foregoing the more important safeguards of popular rights and liberties insofar as they affect the form of government advocated by the Calvinists. There are other measures for the protection of individual rights and liberties of individuals and groups in society which do not concern the question of the form which the government must assume.

12

The Task of the Government

In the famous preamble of the Constitution of the United States, the framers declared the objectives they sought to secure through the government which they were about to inaugurate: "to establish justice, insure domestic tranquility, provide for the common defense, promote the general welfare, and secure the blessings of liberty to ourselves and our posterity." These, and other noble objectives, a good government will seek to obtain through two general lines of activity: (1) the administration of justice and (2) the promotion of the general welfare of the state and of its citizens. Broadly speaking, this is the twofold task of the government according to Calvinistic conception.

The Government and Justice

The first general task of any government is to administer justice. It is the government's business to defend the majesty of the law in human society (Rom. 13:1–4). It is of importance to note that it is God's law which it must administer. In taking this stand, the Calvinist is opposed to such forms of popular sovereignty which make the will of the people the court of last appeal, as if the people could decide what they wished. And Calvinism thereby also stands opposed to all forms of state absolutism, which claim that the state is the court of last appeal, and can decide what it wishes and is answerable to no one.

The Calvinist maintains that God is Sovereign of the universe and that it is his law which the state must administer. Government officials are his ministers, must do his will, and have only so much authority as God has delegated to each of them for their own domain of government.

In order to determine what the will of God is, the state, which is a product of God's common grace and exists in pagan lands as well as in Christian lands, will, in most cases, only have God's revelation in nature as reflected in the human conscience to guide it. But since conscience itself is warped because of sin, and therefore no infallible guide, the state cannot progress properly unless the consciences of its governing officials in the administration of matters of state are guided by the principles of the Word of God. The Word of God, therefore, becomes the ultimate God-ordained standard whereby the will of God must be known, and by which the consciences of state officials, and of citizens as well, must be directed.

The Government and the Law of God

If the Bible, then, is the ultimate criterion by which the state must be guided in determining what laws it must administer, the question arises about how much of the Bible the state must concern itself with. We can state what is in substance the same question in a slightly different form: Since it is the state's business to administer God's law, and since the laws and principles of government which are spread through the whole Bible are summarized for us in the Decalogue, with how much of the Ten Commandments must the state concern itself? It is obvious that the Bible and the Ten Commandments deal not only with the law of the land, but also with the conduct of individuals, the home, the church, and all other groups in human society. The state is only interested in the law of God insofar as it relates to its own sphere of civil government.

It would be incorrect to assert that the state must concern itself only with the second table of the law and not with the first. For, to begin with, the state does not even have a duty toward all the commandments of the second table. The tenth commandment reads, "Thou shall not covet." In civil life a man may covet evil things all he pleases. As long as he does not convert his evil desires into actual deeds, the law of any land will let him go scot free. The reason is that the civil law does not presume to pass upon matters which are purely and only of the heart! Civil law relates to outward conduct. Nor must the state concern itself with the entire field covered by the other five commandments of the second table. There are many matters bearing upon such questions as the relation of parents to children and husbands to wives, and questions of personal honor, which do not concern the state.

It would also be erroneous to maintain that the state, as God's minister, need not concern itself with the first table of the law. Calvin and all the principal religious groups from the time of Constantine, or rather even from the time of the ancient Romans, were indeed wrong when they made the government the defender of the true religion. God never entrusted the propagation and defense of the true religion to the government. He entrusted this task to the church. And the weapons by which it was to be propagated and defended were not the sword of the state and the use of force, but the sword of the Spirit, the Bible, which changes hearts and minds.

But the state may never be atheistic. While it is not the divinely appointed agent to propagate religion, it must demand respect for God the Creator, who is Sovereign in all spheres. It must punish false oaths. It must be interested in the observance of the day of rest as a creation demand for all, even though it does not have as its duty the enforcement of all the religious worship included in the fourth commandment. Even in regard to the question of the morals of its citizens, which has reference to the second table, the state does not have as its duty the maintenance of a full program of morality but only, as it has been termed, the enforcement of an ethical minimum in its citizens for the well being of the state.

The Domain of the Government

We have next an important and vexing problem to consider in determining the task of the state: the extent of the territory over which the state has jurisdiction and in which it must administer justice. In the solution which it offers to this problem, the Calvinist system occupies middle ground between all theories which advocate state absolutism and theories which advocate consistent individualism, as those of the old-time liberalists.

The tendency of state absolutists is to bring everything under the domination of the totalitarian state. According to this view, the state's task would be to govern everything within the territorial limits of the state—a man's personal life, his home, his religion, and the internal affairs of all groups in society. Men and organizations in society would then have only as much liberty as the state would allow them. There never existed a thoroughly totalitarian state. For practical reasons, totalitarian states always allow individuals and groups certain concessions of rights and privileges. Nevertheless, the various forms of state absolutism hold that if the state should choose, it would have the right to direct all matters of all citizens residing within its territory.

The individualistic view of the liberals of former days went to the very opposite extreme. It sought to draw away from the domination of the state as much as it possibly could. According to this view that state governs best which governs least. The ideal condition would be reached if the state could and would bow itself out of existence and leave the individual to himself to run things as he might choose.

In opposition to the first of these two positions, the Calvinist maintains that there are very definite limits to the state's authority. The state is not absolute. It cannot do anything it pleases. First of all, its territory is limited to the province of the natural common good (*bonum commune naturale*). It may not presume to regulate such spiritual matters as the religion of a man's heart, sometimes defined as his conscience. In this area, conscience has not improperly been termed the limit of the state's authority.

A second boundary of the state's authority arises from the nature of the individuals who inhabit the state. The individual is not the mere creature of the state, existing only by and for the state. As God's image-bearer he has duties and responsibilities in his private life beyond the duties he owes to the state for which he must be allowed the necessary freedom and upon which the state may make no encroachment.

A third boundary limiting the state's authority lies in such natural spheres in society as the home, the school, the church, and economic and social organizations, which do not owe their origin or mode of existence to the state, and have their own task entrusted to them by God. These are sovereign within their own boundaries. Only insofar as any of these should overstep its limits, or endanger the welfare of other spheres, or of individuals, or of the state, or insofar as by neglect of its duty it should endanger the well being of the state, has the state here a duty to perform. A case in point would occur when parents neglect the proper training of their children, or when a husband abuses his wife, or one group in society tyrannizes another group.

The Calvinist is equally opposed to the other extreme, that of the individualism of the liberals, which tends to reduce the interference of the government—specifically in economic and social matters—to the barest minimum, and to allow these groups to have their own way unrestrained, letting things take their natural course. The French Revolution had advocated such a laissez-faire policy on the part of the government. But such a policy has in a world of sin constantly led to the oppression of the weaker members of society by the stronger, the exploitation of laborers by unscrupulous capitalists, the tyrannizing of small tradesmen by big business, or groups with power over those who have little or none, and has also led to the decline of various trades and industries through no fault of their own, or of others, but simply because of general conditions which might have been remedied by governmental action.

The Calvinist would not credit the government with the right to step into the separate sphere of economic or social organizations and adopt as a policy the notion that it has the right to own and manage these. Nevertheless, he does believe it to be the duty of the government to administer justice by enacting such regulations as will prohibit any individuals or groups in society from overstepping their proper boundaries, and thereby encroaching in any way on the rights of others or of the state as a whole. And, positively, he believes it to be the duty of the government to provide such regulation of business and other economic and social forces as will bring about better living conditions for all.

The Calvinist found in his Bible proof in abundance for adopting this position. The divine ordinances for the civil administration of the Jewish nation determined not only the procedures of justice in the punishment of crimes such as murder and theft, but also the regulations concerning the taking of interest, proper working conditions and wages of laborers, the rights of the poor to the leavings of the grain and vintage harvest, provisions against the exploitation of the poor by means of the return of the land to the original owners in the year of Jubilee, and other important regulations.

While the Calvinist maintains that these divine regulations for the Jewish nation were not intended for and are not applicable to present-day conditions, yet he does maintain that they embody principles of government which are eternal and should hold everywhere under all conditions and in all ages. Today, too, the government must consider it to be its duty by proper regulation of the economic and social conditions, not alone to counteract existing evils, but positively to promote the most equitable conditions and relations for all concerned.

The laws which the government must enact for the administration of justice are commonly divided into private law (which deals with the relation of individuals and groups to each other) and public law (which deals with the relation of individuals to the state); or civil and criminal law; or, from another point of view, constitutional law (dealing with the principles of law as embodied in the constitution) and common law (unwritten) and statute law (written). In order to accomplish its task of administration of justice, the government will have the duty to frame laws (the legislative branch), to enforce these laws (the executive branch), and to decide in given cases of law (the judicial branch).

The task of the government will not always and everywhere be equally extensive. In an unorganized or semiorganized state of society it will be called upon to perform several tasks which should be done, but either are not done at all or are not adequately done, by the groups in such society; while in a well-organized society, it will have fewer such tasks to perform. Again, in a more complex state of society additional duties will fall to the lot of the government not required under simpler conditions. And in times of national crises the government, in order to protect society from disintegration, will be called upon to exercise powers and assume duties which in normal times it would not have a right to assume.

Besides the duty to administer justice in the affairs of the state internally, there is also the duty of the government to administer justice in the relation of its nation to foreign governments. It will have the duty to protect the state against all invasion of rights and territory by any foreign power. And, as a second main duty toward the outside, it will bear the responsibility, as a member of the family of nations, to help settle questions of international law in the relation of the several states to one another.

The Government and the General Welfare

The task of the government is, however, more extensive than the administration of justice. Its second great task is to promote the general welfare. The general welfare is, to be sure, already advanced by the proper administration of justice. What is meant here is rather such additional activities of the government, apart from administration of justice, as will promote the natural common good—the material, cultural, and philanthropic well being of the members of society in general. As such, additional activities could be cited: the postal service, public utilities, and the development of natural resources, matters which are too general or in other ways cannot properly be cared for by individuals or groups in society. In addition such interests as the lending of aid to industrial, social, or intellectual organizations in society in critical times—either by subsidy or by regulation—become governmental concern when these groups are temporarily weakened and need assistance, as does the giving of aid to sections of the country where disaster has overtaken the inhabitants.

The Calvinist and the Liberal

The Calvinist has never hesitated to ascribe to the government such general tasks dealing with the public welfare. We have abundant evidence of this in the proposals made to the government of Geneva by Calvin. This great leader advocated many measures dealing with material and ideal and philanthropic culture, which he urged the state officials to undertake in addition to the maintenance of law and order. Calvin advocated public loans for the poor and refugees, measures relating to public health, statistical inquiries into the income of districts, the fixing of the price of corn and wine and other commodities, the determination of a proper rate of interest, and even the ownership and operation by the state of a silk industry for the twofold purpose of increasing the revenue of the state and giving added employment to the citizens.[1]

In fact, so much social legislation was enacted by the Genevan government at the time and through the influence of Calvin that his government has been termed Christian socialism. While the government of Geneva was anticommunistic—and thus cannot be called socialism as we know it today—it, nevertheless, stressed emphatically the duty of the government to provide for the public welfare in material, cultural, and philanthropic matters.

Likewise, Abraham Kuyper, who stressed the duty of the government to administer justice, even at times giving the impression that this is the sum total of its duties, nevertheless also attributed to the government such tasks as concern for the public health, the cultural development of society, regulation of child labor, social security, and various other tasks which concern the public welfare. And Hendrik Colyn and the leaders of the Calvinist party in Holland advocated similar measures which concern the public welfare, even enlarging the scope of the state's activities in this regard. Since the current trend toward communism, however, they have been counseling against the dangers of extension of the powers of the government

The Calvinist and the Socialist

It is apparent that in assuming this position the Calvinist takes a stand against the individualism of former liberals. He includes in his program for the government many tasks which are also found in the program of the socialists, such as the ownership and operation of certain public utilities, development of natural resources, social security acts, and even in certain instances, governmental ownership of factories. In fact, long before the socialists of today ever adopted these proposals in their program—in fact, long before Karl Marx ever lived—the early Calvinists (and Calvin himself) already advocated such measures in their program. If, then, the Calvinist has no objection to the public ownership and operation of certain industries, why not go the whole length with the socialist and advocate the public collective ownership of all land and capital and the public collective management of all industries, claiming that it is in the interest of the public welfare to do so? Where lies the line of demarcation, the dividing line between a Calvinist and a socialist?

This dividing line is clearly drawn. The aim of the socialist and of the state socialist is to have society dominated by the state. His ideal is to build up a new society by means of the state. Everything is to be under the direction and control and management of the state. Whatever of particular initiative there will remain, whatever personal or group activities, will only be by the grace of the state.

On the other hand, the Calvinist maintains that the state and society may never be treated as identical concepts. To use a phrase of Woodrow Wilson, society is far broader than the state.[2] Each individual has duties and responsibilities independent of the state for the performance of which he must have his freedom. And the various spheres of society, such as the school, the church, and the economic, social, and intellectual organizations in society have their own God-given circle in which they are individually sovereign. To bring all under the dominance of the state would lead to the suppression of these spheres.

Therefore, while the Calvinist would attribute to the state certain activities in the promotion of the material, intellectual, and philanthropic culture which directly concern all, and calls in the aid of the government for the advancement of the interests of groups in society which either cannot or do not dispatch their duty, the determining principle which differentiates the Calvinist from the socialist is that private initiative must everywhere have the priority. It must be the constant aim of the state to develop these special spheres and to attain more freedom for man to develop his God-given task, not to suppress these spheres or to substitute its own activity for theirs.

For this reason, the Calvinist offers no objection to state ownership and operation of certain industries which directly concern the group as a whole, or where there is imminent danger of a monopoly, as in the case of certain public utilities or natural resources. It has no objection to the fact that the state interest itself in matters of education—even operating educational institutions for the sake of such citizens as would neglect the education of their children—provided it recognize that this duty belongs essentially and first of all to the parent. It has no objection, but rather urges that the state aid the weaker members of society in the economic struggle against the economically stronger members; for example, the employee in the defense of his rights towards his employer, or of the small businessman in his defense against the encroachments of large corporations. Calvinism would have no objection to a tripartite conference between employers, employees, and the government as representative of the public at large which would seek to arrive at equitable wage and working agreements, provided the government so uses its power that these industrial organizations, manufacturers, and labor unions be encouraged in their own initiative rather than suppressed.

It has no objection to state aid for the helpless in human society, or to social security acts, or to provision for superannuated members of society, provided such aids do not tend to crush out private initiative or supersede the work of philanthropic institutions, the church, or private individuals in society. It offers no objection to temporary measures of relief by the government in times of financial depression when individuals, the home, the church, and other relief organizations cannot supply the necessary aid. But these temporary measures may never become permanent, and thereby destroy such relief agencies as are naturally entrusted with the duty of rendering philanthropic assistance to those in distress. The rule everywhere is that private initiative and the activity of the special social unit have the priority, and that, as much as possible, these be advanced rather than destroyed by such measures as the state may choose to take.

Thus we see that the Calvinist has always taken a very different stand than the individualist who would brook little or no interference of the state in economic and social affairs. He also assumes a different position than the socialist and the state socialist who would make the state predominant and rob individuals and organizations in society of their independence.

What the Calvinist desires is such regulation of economic and social conditions by the government as will enable individuals and groups in society to operate as freely as possible, according to their own principle, in their God-given duty in a complex society—while protecting the rights and equity of the other members of society and of the state as a whole. As the history of Calvinistic communities indicates, this is a high ideal that will be ever more closely approximated wherever government officials and citizens seek to be governed by the Word of God and are suffused by the Spirit of Christ.

In its view of the task of the government Calvinism occupies higher ground than any other political theory. Ernst Troeltsch, reflecting upon this aspect of Calvinism, pays it this glowing tribute:

> Calvinism has balanced the two aspects of this antinomy (the relation between the individual and the community) in a very important and powerful manner. . . . Indeed, the great importance of the Calvinistic social theory does not consist merely in the fact, that it is one great type of Christian social doctrine; its significance is due to the fact that it is one of the great types of sociological thought in general. In inner significance and historical power the types of the French optimistic equalitarian democracy, of State Socialism, of proletarian Communist Socialism, and of the mere theory of power, are, in comparison with Calvinism, far behind.[3]

This is indeed a tribute of a high order to Calvinism.

13

The Authority of the Government

This chapter and the next will be devoted to a discussion of the ruler-citizen relationship as this is expressed in the words "authority" and "liberty." These two concepts will occupy a large place in any discussion of the principles of government. When we speak of the prerogatives of rulers, we have particularly in mind their authority, whereas the prerogatives of citizens are associated with their liberties. When the relation between rulers and citizens is as it ought to be, both authority and liberty receive their due rights. Both, however, can be, and in history countless numbers of times have been, abused. Unbridled authority on the part of rulers leads to autocracy, despotism, and tyranny. Unbridled liberty on the part of citizens generates into license, revolution, and anarchy. The puzzling task is to find the proper correlation between these two.

What solution has Calvinism to offer? In settling the problem of individualism and collectivism as this relates to the task of the government, the Calvinist does not obtain his solution by sacrificing either the individual to the community or the community to the individual, but seeks to unite them in a higher unity, wherein both are to promote the will of God in a holy commonwealth. Similarly the Calvinist seeks to preserve both authority and liberty in a higher union found in the observance of the will of God by rulers and subjects alike. Not only authority but liberty as well is achieved by strict adherence to the will of God.

By authority we mean something other than a personal

power that can command influence, respect, or confidence. It here means the right to command and to enforce obedience. A noted physician by his superior learning and skill will enjoy the respect of his colleagues and of the public. But the corner policeman who directs traffic, though far inferior to the physician in native ability, has a right to enforce obedience where the noted physician has not. Whence does the officer derive the authority which he exercises? By nature no man has any right of authority even over a plant or an animal, much less over a fellow man. All men are born free and equal. Whence then does the right to dictate to others and to command their obedience originate?

The Origin of the Government's Authority

Most theories offered in solution of this problem do not go beyond a human origin. They always find the source of authority in man or in something human. It is either the individual, or the state, or the people, or reason, or culture, or simply an impersonal law—always something natural that is supposed to give officials this right to rule. No Calvinist can subscribe to any such theory. For him the source of all authority is always and only God, the Creator, whose creature man is.

Accordingly, Calvinists cannot agree with the philosophy of "natural rights," which teaches that the source of governmental authority out of which these natural rights issue, lies in the state of nature and not in any divine sanction. They also cannot agree with men like Rousseau who held that a social compact lay at the basis of governmental authority. Men were supposed to have agreed to form governments to meet the demands of a more complex society and to delegate to certain men a measure of authority over the rest. Nor can Calvinists accept the theory held by many today, that governments have arisen by evolution out of tribes and tribal customs, and that laws have gradually crystallized. These laws, however, are not supposed to revert to any moral principles behind them. The Calvinists likewise cannot agree with state absolutists who hold that the state is the court of last appeal, the ultimate source which invests rulers with authority. With all who adhere to the Bible, the Calvinists hold that "there is no power but of God. . . . Whosoever therefore resisteth the power, resisteth the ordinance of God. . . . For he [i.e., the government] is the minister of God (Rom. 13:1–4)."[1]

The Duties of Citizens to Their Rulers

The duties which citizens owe to the officials as a result of this authority may be briefly stated as follows: They must have esteem and reverence for authorities as God's ministers (1 Pet. 2:13, 14; Titus 3:1). The Bible denounces all despisers of state officials (2 Pet. 2:10; Jude 8). Second, they must render obedience to the government in all lawful things (Rom. 13:1, 2; Titus 3:1; 1 Pet. 2:13, 14; 1 Tim. 2:1, 2). Citizens must render obedience because government officials are the representatives of God's authority in the sphere of government. Another reason is that obedience is necessary to the proper dispatch of the state's business. Calvin speaks of laws as the soul of the government and urges obedience to the laws as basic to the existence of ordered society. Calvin and Calvinists never tired of stressing this obligation on the part of citizens. Obedience was to be rendered not only to the good and kind rulers, but to "all who possess the sovereignty, even though they perform none of the duties of their function."[2] The reasons for this demand were that God might send evil rulers as punishment and also that citizens may never take the law into their own hands, since private citizens are never vested with governmental authority.

A third duty is to render service to the government. This service implies, first of all, the duty to vote. Wherever this right of franchise is possessed in democratic countries it involves a measure of participation by citizens in deciding policies of the state, a responsibility not given in an absolute monarchy. This service also requires patriotic support of the government. The Bible is insistent that prayers shall be offered for governments, including those that are hostile (1 Tim. 2:1–3). This service further implies participation in the cultural task of the state doing duty as state officials when called on, and rendering military service in time of war. The Calvinists took issue with the Anabaptists on this point.[3]

The Nature of the Government's Authority

It is of importance to have clearly in mind the exact nature of the authority which God delegates to government officials and the method whereby these receive it. The authority which God delegates is never an unlimited one, as state absolutists would claim. Rulers never have a right of absolute and final authority over the entire life of citizens. Their right of rulership is always restricted to their own governmental precincts. The Creator has also delegated a measure of authority to other groups in human society: to parents in the home, to officials in schools and churches, and to heads of corporations in society. Upon this authority, which is likewise delegated by God, the state's officials may not infringe. Their authority is always limited to the dispatch of their own proper functions.

Another important fact to note is that rulers remain God's ministers as long as they are in office. God has not made them his substitutes. He did not relinquish his authority when he appointed them to be rulers. They, therefore, may not govern as they choose, but must administer the affairs of government according to his will. Not the whim of the rulers, nor the will of the majority of the people, nor natural rights, but the ordinance of God is the ultimate deciding factor. With reference to the people, the rule to be observed is that officials must govern for their well being, for that is, as far as human beings are concerned, the reason why God invested those who rule with authority.

Misuse of Authority

Failure to recognize the manner in which rulers receive their authority from God has led to serious error in the past, both on the part of rulers and on the part of the people.

Autocratic kings of former days and their henchmen as, for instance, the Stuarts of England, the Legitimists of France, and the Prussian Junkers of Germany, all abused their rule "by divine right" or "by the grace of God." They falsely interpreted this to mean that the people had no right of control over their actions since they, the rulers, were God's ministers and responsible only to him. The Calvinists, of course, could have no objection to the assertion that kings rule by divine right, insofar as this fact ascribed the source of authority to God. However, this divine right, as Calvinists understood it, operated against all autocratic rule rather than in favor of it. For this divine right to rule was, first of all, not peculiar to kings alone, but was true of every official in state or church or home or school or society. All authority is by the grace of God. This right to rule, furthermore, was not vested in the *persons* of kings, as if these were some sort of higher beings with divine destiny to govern; but this right was inherent in their *office.* The Calvinists taught that even for a prince there cannot be any thought of a *regnum gratia dei* or *droit divin,* any divine right, in any other sense than the one in which each of us exercises divine authority conferred upon us. Kings, therefore, might never rule in an autocratic way, since they are solely God's ministers, delegated to rule the people not for their own pleasure, but for the well being of the citizens and according to the will of God. And the people, as in church so in state, always had the right of control over the actions of the officials.

So insistent were the Calvinists in ascribing all authority and all honor to God as Sovereign that they strenuously opposed all worship of the person of princes and bowing before kings. If God is the great Sovereign, and we all, kings included, are merely creatures of his hand, then to worship the king is a grievous sin, an attack upon the honor due to God. The king is to be honored and obeyed because and insofar as he is invested with authority. A king or ruler, as member of the church, has no higher rank than any private member and is subject to the same discipline.

The Calvinist not only opposed all undue honor to rulers, but likewise opposed the worship or deification of the state or of the head of the state as the one in whom the state was supposed to be personified. The tendency to deify the state has existed in the circle of state absolutists from ancient times on. The Persian despot called himself the sungod and demanded divine homage. Nebuchadnezzar demanded worship for his golden image. Caesar Augustus gave himself the title "Divus Augustus." Religious reverence was demanded for the statue of the emperor. Wherever the theory of state absolutism is in vogue, the tendency runs in the direction of adoration of the head of the state. Antichrist, who will head a world empire, will manifest the same evil trait. He will sit in the temple of God, setting himself forth as God (2 Thess. 2:4). All such deification of the state or of the head of the state is by Calvinists considered a heinous crime against the most high majesty of God and, therefore, is to be strenuously opposed.

While the partisans of former autocratic kings drew one erroneous conclusion from the divine appointment of kings, those who favored popular sovereignty, as did the adherents of the natural-rights theories, drew the very opposite conclusion. These maintained, insofar as they still adhered to the sovereignty of God, that rulers did indeed receive their right to rule from God. However, they did not acquire it directly from God. Rather, it was first given by God to the people who in turn delegated the authority to their chosen officials. The conclusion was that God was the remote Sovereign but that the direct sovereigns were the people. The result was that the concept of God's sovereignty became more remote and the authority of the sovereign people was stressed, until God's sovereignty was frequently eliminated altogether. The people, according to this opinion, appointed their rulers; these were to be the mere executors of the will of the sovereign people and by the sovereign people they might at any time for proper cause be removed.

These theories of natural rights, which have played an important role in the development of modern democracies, are not of Christian or of Calvinistic origin. They were already advocated by ancient classical authors such as Protagoras, Plato, Aristotle, and Cicero. In the Middle Ages adherents of popular sovereignty advocated these views and related them to the sovereignty of God. The Italian Renaissance revived them in the form peculiar to the ancient classical writers. Calvin did not deny the fact that men had natural rights. The Creator has endowed his creatures with certain inalienable rights. However, what these natural rights were could not be definitely determined through natural reason or conscience since these were obscured by sin, but only through the special divine revelation given in Scripture.

It is true, the Bible did teach that rulers are appointed by God through the medium of the people. Even such men as Saul and David, who were at God's command anointed by the prophet to be king, were nevertheless not inducted into office except through the medium of the people. However, the Bible did not teach that the governing authority was delegated first to the people and from them to the officials. This authority came directly upon these chosen officials from God. They were God's ministers, not the ministers of the people. Just as in the church the officials were appointed through the vote of the people, but were nevertheless the ministers of God, so here. What right the people had, both in church and state, was the right of control, that is, the right to pass judgment upon and even lodge necessary complaints against the actions of their rulers.

Later Calvinists, in Scotland and in France, particularly after the severe persecution of St. Bartholomew night, August 24, 1572, deviated from the political theory of Calvin and drifted toward the view that the ultimate human sovereignty rested with the people. Not for every cause but only for the sake of religion may the people, as private citizens, revolt against the government, according to the rule that men ought to obey God rather than men. Hugo Grotius, John Locke, and others went a step further, and virtually departed altogether from the Calvinist view of ultimate divine authority in government. While nominally they still spoke of the authority of God and used scriptural terminology, they grounded the authority of the rulers in the people, not in God. In the French Revolution we see the final disastrous outcome of lodging the ultimate authority in the masses. For the revolutionists overthrew all authority, both divine and human, and on the basis of natural rights sought to defend the right of the populace to revolt and to overthrow authority at their will.

In the American War of Independence the philosophy of natural rights also played an important role in the defense of the right to revolt against the English government. The form in which these concepts of natural rights were here advocated indicates a mixture of Calvinistic and non-Calvinistic ideas. Characteristically, Calvinistic views that were in wide circulation among the colonists were the insistence on the sovereignty of God and natural rights grounded in this sovereignty; the fact that all men are created equal; mutual obligations between rulers and the people; government with the consent of the governed; and resistance by the people to tyranny through responsible representatives. But operating in conjunction with such Calvinistic ideas there were other ideas prominent among them originating in the political theories of Locke, Grotius, Rousseau, and such lesser lights as Barlemaqui, and others. Nevertheless, we find a marked difference in the spirit of revolt among the colonists and the spirit displayed in France during the French Revolution. While in France there was no recognition, but rather an overthrow of the sovereignty of God, among the American colonists it was the reverse, even though the spirit was not all that we could wish it to have been. No less than four national thanksgiving days were declared at the time of the American Revolution: once in 1777 when Burgoyne surrendered; once in 1784 to commemorate peace; again in 1789 when the Constitution was adopted; and again in 1795 when there was a period of general prosperity. All this indicates a conscious recognition of the sovereignty of God and allegiance to him.

From this brief historical reference we glean the following facts regarding the Calvinistic view of the authority of rulers. This authority is received of God. It always remains the authority of God. It is never relinquished by him to the rulers. They remain his ministers. Their authority is restricted to their own domain of government and does not extend to the entire life of the citizens. The home, the church, the school, and other spheres of society each have their own province given them by God to which the authority of the government does not extend and upon which it many not encroach. With respect to the people this rulership must be for their welfare. Government officials are appointed through the people and rule with the consent of the governed. As in church so in state; the people have a right of control. The people must render all due honor, obedience, and service to the government for God's sake. As private citizens the people have never received any governmental authority, have no right to rule, and, therefore, may never take the authority into their own hands or revolt against the duly established government. The most they, as private citizens, may do, and in certain cases must do, is offer passive resistance whenever the officials require anything contrary to their conscience in rendering obedience to the will of God.

The reader can readily understand that such views make for highly stable governments. Citizens must render full obedience to their rulers, out of the highest motives, for God's sake. This gives rise to a very vital question: How, if ever, with such views, can citizens be expected to defend their God-given rights and liberties against rulers who are tyrants? This important question will be given consideration when we discuss Calvinism and civil liberty.

14

Civil Liberty

The topic of civil liberty concerns the rights and privileges of citizens, just as authority involves those of officials.

Citizens have a right to expect definite things of their government. All men have an inward craving for life, liberty, and the pursuit of happiness. Insofar as governments exist for the welfare of the citizens, these have a right to look to them for aid in the accomplishment of these ends. The government has the duty to protect the citizen's material and spiritual existence, to make possible for him his own orbit, in which he can freely move without disturbance or interference unless with good and sufficient reason.

Liberties Due the Citizens

We can perhaps briefly summarize the privileges which the state must guarantee and seek to secure for its citizens under four heads. First of all, citizens—including organized groups of citizens within the territory of the state, such as churches, educational, commercial, and philanthropic institutions—may claim the right of protection by the state from any and all who may seek to encroach upon their legitimate interests.

A second privilege which the citizens may claim refers to special spheres of activity within the state in which a citizen must be engaged. Since the state is not absolute in its power, and the citizen has other duties to perform than the ones which he owes to the state, such as those in the home, the church, and other fields in society, the state may not molest him in the free exercise of these other duties. It must rather seek to promote the conditions and relations which will provide the citizen with the necessary freedom to accomplish his God-given duty in these other realms.

A third duty of the state relates to the citizen's material well being. It is not the business of the state to supply food to its citizens. Emergencies may arise calling for relief measures for the destitute. But the state is not the divine institution designed to feed and clothe human beings. Each man himself is obligated by God to work for his daily food and that of his family. Rather is it the business of the state to establish such conditions as will enable citizens to secure their own living in a manner compatible with human dignity.

A privilege of a very different order which the state must guarantee the citizen relates to his spiritual existence. Just as the state must provide conditions which will tend to promote his material well being and enable him to earn a decent living, so the state must promote his spiritual freedom—freedom for man's soul. This will include freedom of speech, freedom of the press, freedom of religion—in a word, freedom of conscience. This is a cause of which the historic Calvinist is an ardent defender. Calvinists in history have not always consistently practiced this principle in granting liberty of conscience to others; nevertheless, freedom of conscience follows directly from the principles of Calvinism and must strenuously be maintained as a right which the state must grant its citizens. Liberty of conscience may be defined as the boundary line of the state's authority in the realm of the spirit.

The Citizen's Liberties and Despotic Rulers

The state should seek to promote the freedom of its citizens in these four directions. But how are these rights and privileges to be secured and maintained in the case of an autocratic and tyrannous government? If officials are unwilling, how is this political liberty to be promoted? The previous chapter, dealing with the problem of governmental authority, revealed the fact that, according to Calvinistic conception, a person may never in the capacity of private citizen revolt against the government or disobey the laws of the land, not even when hard pressed for the sake of his religion. He may never arbitrarily select which laws he will choose to obey and which not. Strict obedience to the civil magistrates is enjoined by Calvin and Calvinists because of the high motive of obedience to God.

Such cases are cited in proof as that of Jesus, who obeyed an unjust ruler, Pilate, in an unjust cause, recognizing that Pilate was given power over him from above. And the case of Paul is cited, who gave and counseled obedience to an unjust government and who sealed his obedience with martyr's blood. The most that any person as private citizen can and should do when it concerns a matter in which he is directly asked to violate the will of God is to offer passive resistance. Such views, to be sure, promote a stable government, as all can see. But it is not yet clear how a citizen can defend his God-given liberties with such views.

However, this very obedience for God's sake, arising out of the recognition of the magistrates as God's ministers, has operated as a two-edged sword, and has been the mightiest weapon known in history for curbing the tyranny of autocratic monarchs. This same God, who was supreme Ruler, has indicated in his Word a method, not of violence by unauthorized private citizens flouting law and order, but a legal method, whereby unlawful rulership of tyrants is to be duly checked. It was simple enough on the Calvinistic basis to provide evidence of unlawful exercise of authority by autocratic rulers because any violation of the law of God, of the king's coronation oath, or of the constitution made the ruler remiss in his duty, and hence an authority to be resisted. But the important question was how? The method whereby this resistance was to be effected and the rights and liberties of the people defended was by constitutional resistance through the legal representatives, termed by Calvin the inferior magistrates. In all governments we have not only the supreme rulers but such lesser authorities as councilors, estates, parliaments, and congresses. These inferior magistrates, so Calvin argued, are set by God for the defense of the rights of the people against irresponsible rulers. "If they connive at kings in their oppression of their people, such forbearance involves the most nefarious perfidy, because they fraudulently betray the liberty of the people, of which they know that they have been appointed protectors by the ordination of God."[1] Wherever opposition to autocracy through such legal representatives was not possible, Calvin counseled submission rather than popular revolt. The case of Calvin's advice against the conspiracy at Amboise in his correspondence with the French admiral Coligny is a notable instance. The bitterly persecuted French Calvinists disregarded Calvin's advice, only to come to grief and have occasion to regret the ill-advised revolt.

The history of Calvinism, on the other hand, offers noteworthy examples of the success of legal methods of resistance to tyranny, notably the revolution of Holland in 1568, of England in 1688, and of America in 1776.

Another method of resistance to tyranny endorsed by Calvinists is the right of intervention by foreign rulers. Calvinists believe in the solidarity of the human race. All nations together form one human family. If subjects of one nation are oppressed and persecuted by their rulers, it becomes the duty of other nations to aid the oppressed, as did Prince William of Orange in Holland.

It will be noted that Calvin, followed in this by the best opinion of Calvinists, did not contribute anything to the right of revolution by private citizens. The Calvinistic political party in Holland even takes delight in naming itself the Anti-Revolutionary party. But Calvin found in the existing inferior magistrates occasion for legal and orderly resistance to tyrants. This resistance was not prompted by a conviction of mere "natural rights," but by divine right. The result has been that, although Calvin has been a stabilizing influence to good government and never preached revolution but rather opposed it, he nevertheless did make tyrants tremble on their throne and sounded the deathknell of their autocracy.

Calvinism and Political Liberty

The following general facts will help us to evaluate properly the contribution which Calvinism has made to modern liberty. The thirst for liberty did not arise with Calvinism. It is as old as the human race. Moreover, other nonreligious factors have contributed to the development of modern liberty, notably economic and political factors. It is also important to note that the doctrine of natural rights, which played so crucial a role in the struggle for modern liberty, did not originate with the

Calvinists but was already asserted by the ancient Greeks. But Calvinism did two things with respect to these doctrines of natural rights: (1) it correlated the natural rights theories with the basic idea of the sovereignty of God and the authority of Scripture; and (2) it converted these teachings of natural rights, which with others lacked sufficient power to effect the necessary reforms, into working principles for the assertion of the rights of citizens and the defense of liberties over against the tyranny of governments. It was chiefly after and through Calvinism that these theories of natural rights became effective. As Ernst Troeltsch asserts, Calvinism was the spiritual backbone of the movement for modern political liberty. What positive English law, economic forces, skeptic toleration, and literary declarations could not achieve was made possible through the religious convictions of the Calvinists. Their religious convictions prompted them to action and made them the spiritual backbone of the political liberties of their countries.[2]

It is also important to note that Roman Catholicism, Arminianism, Lutheranism, and even Zwinglianism were either monarchistic in their tendency and in their form of church government, or at least, as in the case of the Lutherans and Zwinglians, found it in their best interest to support the crown. Calvinism was the great germinal spiritual power of modern democracy. Along with Calvinism must be listed such independent sects as the Baptists and Quakers. These have, both in England and America, had a determinative role in the battle for political liberty. It must be remembered, however, that these groups, although theologically deviating in certain points from the Calvinists (Roger Williams remained a Calvinist until his death, except in the matter of infant baptism), nevertheless, politically took a stand which was an outflow of the Calvinistic theory and spirit.

Although the Roman Catholic, Lutheran, and Arminian views all linked the church with the state, the Calvinistic theory furnished the only effective system in the Reformation age for the organization of oppressed Protestantism. Calvinism made possible a church that was free from state control, thus giving rise to free and independent thought. Williston Walker, in speaking of this aspect of Calvinism, cites Scotland, where in the latter part of the sixteenth century the Scottish General Assembly was a truer embodiment of the people's wishes than the Scottish parliament.

The manner in which the Calvinistic churches were organized contributed its part—in fact an important part—to the development of the spirit of political liberty among the Calvinists. Whether one takes the Presbyterian form or the Independent form of church government as developed by the Calvinists, in each case the government of the local church—the basic unit of church government—was in the hands of the minister and elders, chosen by the people. Thus the power over the church was given into the hands of the laity. This, as Walker tells us, made every Calvinistic parish a school of government in a sense not true of any other communion in the Reformation age. The elders were rulers chosen by the vote of the people and served only with the consent of the congregation by whom they were elected. If such organization was possible in the holiest of all institutions on earth, the church, why not, so the Calvinist argued, also in the state? Why not elect kings and magistrates in the same way? Scotland, England, and America asked that question, and the answer is written large in the annals of the seventeenth century.[3]

The strict adherence of the Calvinist to the Bible and the unrestricted influence which he gave it over his life also added markedly to the promotion of a spirit of liberty. This, however, is true, not only because the Calvinist wanted freedom to worship his God according to the precepts of the Bible. While the Bible, indeed, was to him the only way of salvation, it meant much more to him than a way of salvation. It embodied the principles which must control his whole life. As the Calvinist argued the right of compacts and of constitutions, he studied his Bible and found that even such men as had been anointed by God to be rulers over Israel, notably Saul and David, were made kings in no other way than by a compact and through the medium of the people. And when the Calvinist felt called upon to resist tyrannous princes, he noted that in the case of Jeroboam the son of Nebat and the godless kings who succeeded him and made Israel to sin, stern rebuke was given by God to Israel for not opposing these kings but following in their sins. To the Calvinist this was an example of the duty which devolved upon subjects when rulers would lead them away from the law of their God.

Another important factor in the promotion of political liberty was the conviction of the sovereignty of God. On the one hand, this controlling thought made the Calvinist a law-abiding citizen, with profound regard for the political authority placed over him, because he saw in it the authority of his God. But on the other hand, kings were as obligated to obey this sovereign God as the meanest subject in the land, and the inferior magistrates were appointed to see to it that they did. The fact that kings ruled by the grace of God operated as a two-edged sword which counteracted the autocratic power of despots.

Even the view of man's total depravity, in which the Calvinist was a firm believer, aided the spirit of liberty. For this total depravity had made its inroads in all humanity, in kings as well as subjects. As a result, while the Calvinist saw a representative of God in the king as ruler, in his personal life the king was nothing more than a sinner like all others. Conversely, the Calvinist confessed that though he as citizen was also a sinner and needed the grace of God, yet by that grace he had become a son of the living God, of spiritual nobility, of royal blood, a match for kings and nobles, enabled by the grace of God to do all things.

Last but not least, if you are to understand why the Calvinist has been a potent factor in the advancement of political liberty, you must keep in mind the great doctrine of election, which in these sturdy days of historic Calvinism operated as a mighty dynamic force, impelling him on to high moral duty as a man called of God. He felt himself called not only to salvation in eternity, but to defend God's cause in the whole of life. The result of this faith in divine election was immense. As Henry Ward Beecher says, "He who believes in election knows himself chosen for some end, to attain which is his moral calling, a calling for the sake of which, since it is divine, life's most precious thing, if need be, must be sacrificed, but a calling also, in which success is certain, since God, Who is Sovereign, called him unto it. Such facts have always made the Calvinists the staunchest and bravest defenders of freedom."[4]

The beauty of the Calvin-founded civil liberty—a fact especially to be noted—lies in this, that it proceeds along the lines of law and order and carries with it respect for authority, something which cannot be said of the type of political liberty engendered by religious indifference and skepticism, as we find it exemplified in the leaders of the French Revolution. Any democracy that fails to take into account the sovereignty of

God must be unstable, as the numerous revolutions through which France has since passed and the turbulent conditions of the revolutionary South American republics indicate. Compare the countries where civil liberty has been enjoyed in the form advocated by Calvinism, such as England, Holland, and the United States, and the difference is marked. The statement once made by Saint Augustine, *Deo servire, vera libertas,* "to serve God, this is true liberty" is a word after the heart of the Calvinist. To make democracy safe for the world, it needs, as the Calvinist strenuously insists, a high regard for the sovereignty of God.

15

The Sovereignty of the Social Spheres

The previous chapter emphasized the relation of the government to the private citizen. The present chapter discusses the relation of the government to the organic groups of citizens in society.

An expression which has become a favorite watchword among Calvinists is, "The sovereignty of the organic groups in society each in its own sphere." By this is meant that the family and scientific, commercial, industrial, agricultural, and philanthropic organizations, and whatever other groups naturally develop out of the organic life of human society, as well as churches, do not owe their origin, existence, or principle of life to the state. They have an inner principle and cultural task all their own, entrusted to them by God. They are authorized directly by God for the pursuance of their task. Upon this sovereignty given them by the Creator the state may not infringe.

The problem of the relation of the government to various groups in society is age-old. Especially the matter of the relation which the government must sustain to one of these groups, namely, to the church, is a moot question and has given rise to endless controversies. The ancient pagan nations were already vexed with this problem, as the friction of the pharaohs with the priests of Egypt and of the caesars of Rome with the vestal virgins indicates. During the Middle Ages the church and the state divided the whole of human society between them. These two institutions considered themselves man's overlords. They kept vying with each other for supremacy, with now the state and then the church being accorded the ultimate sovereignty. Toward the dawn of the modern period a third circle, distinct from both state and church, began to assert itself and demand a measure of independence, namely society. This was especially noticeable in the economic and scientific areas of society. Universities, guilds, and business organizations began to assert their independence and claim for themselves sovereign rights in their respective domains upon which neither state nor church might infringe. The struggle of these groups for the maintenance of their liberties from dominance of either state or church occupies a large and interesting page in modern history. At the present time the absolutism of such governments as Soviet Russia, Red China, and Yugoslavia has brought the problem to the foreground. The increased attention given to the state-church relation in books and magazines and at religious gatherings is largely explained by this fact.

The question of the relation of the state to the church, while important enough in itself, is after all only a part of this major problem of the relation of the state to any and all organic groups in society which operate upon an inner principle of their own. The solution which one offers to this major problem will, in a large measure, be determinative for his answer to the problem of the relation of the state to that unit within the territory of the state, which is known as the church.

The solution which the Calvinist offers is not determined by mere practical considerations out of a bias in favor of either church or state, or a preference for individualism or collectivism. The Calvinist considers all lawful organizations—whether state, or church, or organic associations in society—as God-established and, therefore, deserving of their due rights. The solution is to be solely determined by the respective places which these organizations are designed, according to the divine economy and Holy Writ, to occupy in human society.

The Sovereignty of the Social Spheres

Calvinism views society not as a loose aggregation of isolated individuals, but as an organic unity, one vast social organism.

This organism is composed of a wide variety of distinct though related spheres, which arise out of the complex life of mankind, each having its own task to perform, its own mandate entrusted to it by God. Thus there is the sphere of the family, of science, of art, of technique and invention, of trade and commerce, of industry, of agriculture, of the church, and, to mention no more, the sphere of things which belong to society as a whole.

As each of these spheres has been authorized and commissioned by God to carry out its specific task, it has therefore sovereign rights within its own domain. No outside influence, whether of state or church or other social unit, may interfere with the proper pursuance of this task by the group itself, without thereby infringing upon the authority which God has delegated to that group. This is what is known as the sovereignty of the spheres of society. Had human life remained normal with no sin to disrupt society, each group would have gone about its task without interference from other social units and in full harmony with them, without the need of a government as we know it today. Through the harmonious activity of all the social bodies, man's cultural task in a great kingdom of God would have been realized.

It is of importance to note the exact nature of the authority which is exercised by men in these spheres. The authority comes to them in a natural, organic way, not mechanically, as in the case of governmental authority. No parent exercises authority over his child because he was voted into the office of parent. No scientist speaks with authority in his field merely because men have appointed him to that position. Their authority is natural to them in their field.

An examination of a few of these spheres will clarify this issue. Already in the orbit of the individual this fact is true. Any mastery which one man by virtue of his personality will exercise over other men is due to native talents which he possesses. All personalities are not the same. Some are weak, others strong. The stronger have a natural superiority which makes them respected by the rest. Although this holds true as a general statement, the force of it is felt particularly in the case of those superior personalities who are geniuses in some definite field. The man who has special talent as a technical expert, or as a scientist, or as an artist, naturally has something about him that commands respect. People bow to his authority and recognize him as a master without any appointment to office. Every artist is a priest in the temple of art by virtue of his own right.

What is true of the authority of individuals is equally true of the authority of the organic spheres in society. In a family the authority over the group affairs of the home is not received by appointment from some outside power, for example the state, but comes naturally to the head of the family, the parent. In a scientific organization, such as a school or university, no state can rightfully dictate the scientific conclusions to which such an institution must come. But the laws which are to be enforced are the laws inherent in the sphere itself. And the administration of the school naturally falls to those who are at the head of such a scientific organization as scientific leaders. Likewise in a business organization no set of arbitrary governmental rules and regulations can promote business, but only business rules apply. And again, the proper individuals to conduct a business are the heads of the commercial organization. Agriculture similarly does not receive its laws from the government, but must obey the laws of nature. And so it is in all spheres. Whenever any government presumes to determine the natural laws of operation in these spheres, those working in such spheres grow restive and protest against what they consider to be illegitimate interference in the internal workings of their field. Such facts clearly indicate that there is a natural sovereignty given to these domains of which men are instinctively conscious.

In the case of the church there is a difference in the manner in which this social body originated. The church did not arise, as the other spheres, out of the normal life of creation. In fact, had life developed normally without sin, there would have been no church any more than there would have been a state in the present sense of the term. For the church arose as a result of sin and is an institution of God's special grace. Nevertheless, in both instances, the church, as well as the other spheres in society, has its own task with a corresponding authority assigned by God, upon which no state or other outside power may infringe. In fact, in the case of the church, the authority is even more specifically safeguarded than that of any other sphere. We are expressly and repeatedly told that in the sacred body of the church, Christ, and he only, is sovereign. When states have presumed to exercise authority over the church, whether in early church history or at the present time, the blood of martyrs has flowed freely to defend the sovereignty of the church from state domination.

There is still a fifth group which has a sphere and a task of its own in the cultural life of society, distinct from that of the individual, the family, corporations in society, and the church. It is the community itself or society as a whole. There are certain common cultural tasks which belong to none of the separate spheres individually but are the work of society as a whole, since they concern them all in common. For the direction of these tasks there must be appointed responsible agents of the entire group.

The Civil Government and the Social Spheres

What now is the relation of the sovereignty of the state to the sovereignty of the spheres? Ideally there is no conflict between the sovereignty of the several spheres and that of the government. They all derive their authority from a common source, namely, God. And in each the sovereignty is delegated by God directly to the unit which is to exercise it, not through the medium of another sphere.

There is, however, a distinct difference in the manner in which political governments have arisen and the purpose for which each exists, as also in the method by which authority is to be exercised. All social groups, with the exception of the church, have developed in an organic way out of the normal life of humanity. Not so the government. In fact, if life had developed normally, without the interruption of sin, there would have been no state or government as we know them. There would have been a kingdom of God in which all humanity would have been united. However, this kingdom of God is today not continued in our present state, but in Christ's spiritual kingdom found in the church. The state with its legislative, executive, and judicial branches of government, its armies, navies, and police force is an institution of God's common grace, a mechanical device called into being because of sin and instituted to curb sin's violence and make possible an ordered society. That this is the reason why governments exist is clearly taught in Scripture, notably in Romans 13:1–6, and explained in article 36 of the Belgic Confession. The civil government, therefore, since it did not arise from the natural organic life of man, as did the family or the sphere of science, does not have to perform a peculiar cultural task ordained at creation. Its task is due to sin. It must administer justice in a sinful world for the punishment of evildoers and for the praise of them who do well.

The fact that the civil government is a mechanical device of God's common grace to permit the fulfilment of the cultural task of the spheres of society in a world of sin indicates clearly the duty which the government has with respect to these spheres. It does not have the duty to take over the work of these spheres, as is the tendency in a totalitarian or collectivist state. That would tend to annihilate rather than to promote and aid these groups in their God-given tasks. Nor may the government allow them to operate unrestrained according to their sinful desires, as the laissez-faire policy of the liberals would demand. That would be to shirk a great part of the duty which the state is called upon to perform in a sinful society, namely, to administer justice.

It is rather the business of the state, negatively, to counteract whatever forces would tend to break down the normal operation of the several spheres of society in their God-given task; and, positively, to promote such conditions and relations as will be helpful to them in the pursuance of their cultural tasks. In abnormal circumstances it may even for the time being become the duty of the state to subsidize, or even temporarily to assume the duties of some of the weaker groups, in order to bring them back to their normal state. But amid all the multifarious and diverse duties which the state may be called upon to assume toward the social spheres, this must always be the guiding rule: The interest of the social spheres must have the priority. The organic authority delegated by God to the spheres precedes the mechanical authority of the state. No civil government may presume to ignore, alter, or destroy the divine commission given to each sphere to perform its God-given task. In the last analysis the family, science, art, industry, and agriculture do not exist for the benefit of the state, but the state exists for the well being of these spheres. That is why God called it into existence.

Briefly stated, the duty of the government toward the social spheres would be: (1) to prevent possible conflicts between the various units and to promote conditions whereby each can operate as freely as possible in its God-given task; (2) to protect individuals and whatever is weak within these social groups against abuse of power by the stronger elements; and (3) to demand of all whatever personal and financial duties may be necessary for the preservation of the state.

There is one other task which Calvinists have always assigned to the civil government, distinct from the task of administration of justice. The preceding discussion has indicated that the state is a mechanical device, arising from the fact of sin, to preserve law and order. That is the specific purpose why, in God's common grace, governments have been called into existence. There are, however, certain general cultural tasks which society as a whole must perform, certain common interests which concern society as a whole, that have nothing to do with administration of justice and that call for a general functioning body to perform them. As such general tasks which have nothing to do with the promotion of justice may be cited the laying of roads and other means of transportation, postal service, development of natural resources, and analogous duties. While a special group of officials other than state officials might conceivably by appointed to represent society as a whole, this would require two sets of officials, the one for the administration of justice, the other to perform the general tasks of society. Calvinists from Calvin's time on have never hesitated to assign such general tasks to the civil government. In the absence of normal representatives of society as a whole, there is no reason why the state should not function in that capacity.

16

The Relation of Church and State

Calvinists believe that the sovereignty of God must be recognized in all spheres of life, including the sphere of government. The will of God, by which men are to be governed, is revealed to us in the Word of God. Although it is true that God originally had revealed his will in nature, specifically by writing that will on the tablets of man's heart, today man has by nature and if from nature only, a blurred impression of what God requires. All his natural impressions must, therefore, be corrected and guided by the revealed will of God found in the Bible. It follows that for the state as well as for the church the eternal principles which are embedded in the Word of God are the norm by which it is to be directed and form the common basis of both state and church.

A problem of no mean importance is the determination of how this will of God, found in the Bible, is to be known by the officials of the state. It is not brought to them directly, as it was in Israel. Calvinists, from Calvin's time on, never hoped to erect a theocracy as in Israel, all that has been said about the supposed theocracy at Geneva notwithstanding.[1] Such an attempt would ignore the special position which Israel was intended to occupy in the family of nations. Nor is the will of God to be communicated to state officials through the medium of any church or denomination. In sacerdotal circles, such as the Roman Catholic Church, where the church is placed between the individual and his God as the official interpreter of God's will, such views would be natural. But the Protestant believes in the right of private judgment. Moreover, the Calvinist believes in the sovereignty of each sphere in matters of its own domain. Hence, each man is called upon by God to interpret the Bible for himself and each sphere for itself. The eternal principles of the Word of God are to be arrived at, not directly, as in Israel, or through the medium of any church or ecclesiastical body, but through the consciences of both the government officials and the citizens.

It is important to note that this is something very different than the assertion that the consciences of state officials or of the citizens are the guiding rule in civic affairs, as if the opinions of political leaders or of the people are the court of last appeal by which matters of state are to be decided. Though the consciences are the means, they are not the end. The objective and unassailable norm for civic affairs is and remains the Word of God. But this is to be determined through the consciences of the officials and citizens.

It is indeed a fact that when political leaders become unbelievers, they are not open to influences from the Word of God. But God remains Sovereign of the state nevertheless; his ordinances, and the duty of governments to conform to these ordinances, remain. This is a conviction which the Christian may never yield without becoming unfaithful to his God and to his Christian confession. As a result, it is a great duty of Christian citizens to operate as a leaven in the state. Wherever these have faithfully performed their duty, so history reveals, conformity by the state to the revealed will of God has been promoted. Today, in lands where Christianity is a potent force, the state dare not inaugurate if it would, except at great risk, certain measures which run counter to the consciences of its Christian citizens.

Differences between the State and the Church

There is, therefore, a common basis for state and church in the Word of God. This fact will insure the necessary harmony and aspiration for common and lofty ideals. But together with this common basis, there is also a very marked difference between the two spheres of state and church. The church does not owe its rise to the state, but acknowledges Christ as its

Source and King, has its origin in regeneration and special grace, deals with spiritual matters, and has as its purpose the building up of the body of Christ and the spiritual kingdom of God. The state, on the other hand, has its origin in natural life as it has existed after the fall, belongs to the sphere of common grace, deals with earthly relations, and finds its purpose in the maintenance of law and order in human society and in the *bonum commune naturale.*

The relation between these two spheres should be one of harmony and cooperation. Both are institutions of God; both as institutions are intended to curb sin, the one in the sphere of common grace, the other in the sphere of special grace; both are designed positively to promote the ethical ideal of society and thus advance the kingdom of God, the one indirectly by removing hindrances from the pathway of the church in establishing this kingdom, the other directly. Both state and church as institutions will cease to exist at the end of time, while the church as a living organism and the kingdom of God, established through supernatural means, will continue throughout eternity. These two institutions should, therefore, labor for the realization of their God-given tasks in the greatest possible harmony.

Duties of the State to the Church

Accordingly, the duties of the state to the church may be conveniently grouped under the following four heads. First of all, the state may not be neutral with respect to religion in general. Such a position would make the state virtually atheistic and would violate the sovereignty of God in all walks of life. The state should recognize the existence of and its responsibility to God. This we are happy to note, is done in the Declaration of Independence, where it is stated that "the Creator has endowed His creatures with certain inalienable rights." The attempt is made at times to prove that the Constitution is committed to a purely secular philosophy. But the evidence points rather in the opposite direction. The founders of our country were for the greater part Christians and desired to keep their country so. But they were unwilling to curtail the liberties of the constituent states, and therefore did not want to commit the country to any particular form of Christianity. The state has the duty to promote the honor of God, to protect the church, and to observe and foster the observance of the moral law of God, insofar as this relates to its own proper sphere. Toward its citizens, especially in times of moral decline, it will seek to encourage respect for God's law.

On the other hand, a state may never establish a state church of whatsoever form. Such an act would be to overstep its own proper boundary. The state is not the God-given institution for the propagation of religion. Its duty lies within its own domain of maintaining law and order in human society and of promoting the natural common good. It would also be an infringement upon the rights of the church, which is sovereign in its own orbit and can recognize no authority over it save Christ its King. The establishment of such a state church would also be a violation of the right of private judgment and freedom of conscience in matters of religion. It would also be a retrogression to a former lower level of religion. Even if an ideal condition in religion could be attained in any given country; namely, that all citizens would think alike in matters of religion and would maintain perfect religious standards—which is impossible in this imperfect world where we all know in part—even then it would not be the business of the state to establish a state church, since these two institutions have each received a distinct orbit from God in which they are to operate and the church may never be an arm of the state. But the establishment of a state church in this dispensation would also virtually be a step backward, a retrogression. For it is a common fact of history that nations of antiquity started out with one state church. But as civilization and learning advanced, it became increasingly impossible to corral all men within the confines of a single church. They just did not think alike on basic matters of religion. And the establishment of such a state religion became nothing short of coercion and persecution in matters of conscience.

The state is to have authority with respect to the church only insofar as it concerns matters *circa sacra,* not *in sacra,* which means that the state shall have authority with regard to the externalities of the church, its buildings and other properties, and afford it the same protection under the law as any organization in society within the confines of the country. But the state may never exercise authority *in sacra* by assuming the right to frame laws determining the religious views of its citizens or the government of the church. Whenever the power of the state has been employed for the propagation or control of religion, it has usually turned out to be to the detriment of religion and of the church. The proper God-established means for the propagation of the faith is not the sword of the state, but the gospel, the Word of God, the sword of the spirit.

The state can best aid religion by doing three things which in a sense are negative in character. It can remove stumbling blocks from the way of the free development of the churches. It can aid by not promoting a counter-religion. It can render service by not propagating religion by force.

Freedom of conscience and, hence, freedom of religion should be guaranteed to all citizens, including unbelievers. No one should be molested by the state because of his religious convictions unless the authority of the state in its own proper sphere is transgressed. Calvinism, from the time of Calvin on, has made much of the freedom of conscience. Calvin also fought a battle for years in Geneva for the complete separation of church and state, though he never achieved his goal. This in time would have led to freedom of religion as its logical outcome. It is true, later Calvinists in Holland, Scotland, and the New England states reverted to a form of state church. Their action might conceivably be defended on the practical ground that the Protestant religion would have gone down in defeat in those turbulent days of the religious wars had not the states taken upon themselves the defense of the Protestant faith. But the establishment of a state church was, nevertheless, a departure from Calvinism as propounded by Calvin. Roman Catholics, Lutherans, and Arminians defended the state church idea as a matter of principle. Not so the Calvinists. Philip Schaff states that in that darkest chapter of church history, the Calvinists were less intolerant than men of other faiths; but they were all intolerant.[2] It is true that freedom of conscience as it manifested itself in the right of free speech was granted to Roman Catholics, Lutherans, and even men of antithetical philosophical opinions like Spinoza in Holland, a privilege which was denied in countries dominated by other faiths; but the right to gather for religious worship and the right of franchise was at times denied by the Calvinists. However, we can thankfully record that it is a principle inherent in Calvinism and today commonly applied, that all churches, all religious societies, and all citizens, irrespective of their views regarding eternal matters, shall be treated on a basis of equality by the state. Religious toleration granted to other than state churches, as exemplified in the constitutions of Italy, Denmark, and the Scandinavian countries, is not identical with complete religious liberty. The Calvinist stands for complete religious liberty to all and religious equality before the state.

Duties of the Church to the State

Not only has the state a duty to fulfil to the church. The church has likewise a very vital duty to fulfil to the state. No ecclesiastical body should presume to dictate how a state should fulfil its God-given duty. Such a procedure would be an encroachment upon the domain of the state, a lording it over the state. It would also involve the difficulty that one church, as state church, would become the official interpreter of the will of God to the state. The state is to be guided by its own God-given conscience in determining what God's Word demands for matters relating to its own domain as state. What churches in an official way may do with respect to the state is well summed up for us in the Westminster Confession (art. 31, sec. 4): "Synods and Councils are to handle or include nothing but that which is ecclesiastical; and are not to intermeddle with civil affairs which concern the commonwealth, unless by way of humble petition in cases extraordinary; or by way of advice for satisfaction of conscience, if they be thereunto required by the civil magistrates."

In addition to this, the church may rightly exert only an indirect influence upon the state, by affecting the consciences of its citizens and officials. The more the consciences of officials and citizens are Christianized, the greater will be the conformity in matters of religion and morals by the state to the law of God. This Christianizing influence should proceed along the following lines: (1) The church in the preaching of the gospel must enunciate the principles of the Word of God as these apply to all relationships of life, including the political. (2) Christian men of science, Christian colleges, and Christian universities should develop on a Christian basis the principles of the Bible as these relate to civic life. (3) The Christian press, and with it the Christian radio and rostrum, must seek to influence and win public favor for the truths of the Word of God.

17

Internationalism in History

By internationalism we here understand the relations of one nation to another or to the nations generally. These foreign relations must be regulated by moral and judicial norms or rules, just as well as the relations of individuals and institutions within any one nation. The code of laws that governs nations in their interrelations to each other is known as international law.

The Classical and Medieval Periods

In the study of our principles as they bear upon these international relations, it will be helpful to have before our minds the more important trends of thought which have governed nations in their conduct to one another. There is not much of interest to our purpose before the time of the ancient Greeks. Although there were world empires in earlier epochs, they do not afford much light for a theoretical study of internationalism. Even the Greeks were on the whole not internationally minded. The Greeks were by nature individualists, devoted to their own city-state, and interested themselves in the study of philosophy, art, and the humanities. At best they were nationalists. Socrates, who prided himself on being a world citizen, was in that respect an exception to the rule. The cosmopolitan spirit was first developed among them on a large scale by the

Stoics. These spoke of a universal natural law grounded in reason which should govern all men alike, and advocated the view that there should be only one state, one law, and one system of justice for all.

This theory of the Stoics was more sympathetic to the law-loving Roman than to the Greek. It was adopted by Cicero in his system of law and in time became the dominant view of the Romans. In the Roman Empire, in which every inhabitant ultimately received the status of Roman citizen, a system of universal law was developed with the Stoical principles as a basis. The *Corpus juris civilis* of Justinian has influenced political institutions down to modern times.

When Christianity entered and finally conquered the Roman Empire, it became the established universal religion. It also fell heir to the world empire. Christianity in its very nature was not a tribal religion but cosmopolitan. By its moral teaching of the unity of the human race and the brotherhood of all Christians, it greatly aided the spirit of internationalism. John Bassett Moore even states that "the law of nations (international law) was originally the product of the Christian States of Europe."[1] The Christian leaders in the Middle Ages popularized the view that Christianity was not only to control the religion of the church, but the political organization of the state as well. In fact they went so far as to maintain that, just as there was a universal church, so there must be one universal state, the empire. This view was clearly set forth when Charlemagne (A.D. 800) became the political head of the Holy Roman Empire with the pope as Christ's vicar on earth. Theoretically this view was defended by the doctrine that God was the universal Sovereign, and political government on earth was to reflect this fact in one unbroken empire as a unity. And historically the claim was made that the head of the Holy Roman Empire was the rightful successor and heir of the caesars and of their prerogatives. The Roman Empire, and later the Holy Roman Empire, degenerated and in practice did not control the whole of the Western world. Nevertheless, the theory of a universal empire continued to exert a dominant influence up to the thirteenth century, in fact, until the time of the Renaissance and the Protestant Reformation, and exercised a measure of influence even up to the nineteenth century.

The Modern Period

However, as states became politically independent of the empire and of the pope, the theory of the one world empire declined, and with it also the spirit of internationalism; and a spirit of nationalism and of a community of independent states took its place. The Peace of Westphalia in 1648, by the recognition of the independent states, put an end politically to the thought of a world empire, though the spirit of internationalism still found wide adherence until the eighteenth and the nineteenth centuries. Modern science of international law commonly speaks of Hugo Grotius (d. 1645, author of *De jure belli et pacis*) as its founder. With the establishment of the independent states, a new view of nationalism in conjunction with a new set of corresponding ideas takes its place. The dominant factor in the relation between the independent states now becomes, not righteousness, but the balance of power; the nation becomes the supreme unit, is autonomous, recognizes no power above it, and feels itself obligated to observe only such compacts and treaties as it agrees to make and deems fit to keep. The theory of nonintervention becomes popular, imperialism and the exaltation of the individual state receive prominence, and all too often, not justice, but the right of the strongest prevails.

As we approach current history there arises again a growing spirit of internationalism. The close interrelation of nations politically and economically fosters the consciousness of a need of more efficient regulation of international relations. This has led to several international conventions and peace conferences, including The Hague Peace Conference (1899), the second Geneva Convention (1906), the second Hague Conference (1907), the League of Nations (1920), and the present United Nations.

We should not conclude, however, that the views of those favoring well-regulated international relations are today universally adopted. This is far from being the case. In fact, the progress of international law is decidedly uphill work. The recent disappointments of the United Nations seem to indicate retrogression rather than progress. The field today is very much divided between internationalists and nationalists.

Prominent among those who favor a spirit of internationalism are the socialists. In their materialistic philosophy, the possession or nonpossession of this world's material goods is the basic idea which underlies everything. There is a constant class struggle between the "have-nots" and the "haves," the proletariat and the capitalists. They have no real sympathy for nationalistic ideas, at least not in theory. There is to them more affinity between the proletariat of all lands than between the proletariat and the capitalists of any one country. The proletariat have no fatherland. Their slogan is rather "Proletariat of all lands, unite in a common struggle against all capitalists." In practice there is always more sympathy for the specific nation in which they live than their theory would allow, as human nature will tend to dominate theory. But the spirit which they foster is a spirit of internationalism to the neglect of national interests.

There are others who cultivate a spirit of internationalism with a similar disregard for national interests. They do so, however, for a very different reason than the socialists. In their case it is a superficial, not to say false cultural view, which leads them to ignore nationalistic ideas and promote internationalism. These argue that, as civilization advances, the differences which now separate one group in society, and one locality, and one nation from another are destined to fade out and disappear. As a result all national limitations and differences are, after a fashion, hindrances to the progress of civilization and should be eliminated. The more men become civilized the more, so they hold, men become like each other the world over. Provincial habits of dress and provincial customs disappear as civilization advances. Just as in religion all sects and denominations should be superseded by a universal religion and one church, so in the political world individual states should give way to a universal empire with one language (Esperanto), one system of education, and uniform habits and customs. Although these theorists have an eye for the common elements which should exist in men because all are members of the one human race, they fail to see that in the cultural task of humanity distinct individuals and distinct peoples each have a specific task to perform for which they have been endowed by their Creator, and for which they need sovereignty each in its own sphere. The uniformity for which they strive would only bring about a superficial unity, a veneer, and would disregard the national and other distinctions which lie deeper and are necessary for the development of a healthy internationalism.

Still others favor internationalism at the expense of nationalism, not on rational but emotional grounds. Several of the ultrapacifists can be classified here. These point to the terrible disputes, the dissensions, the economic struggles, and the wars which arise between the various nations, and see in the one vast world empire a solution which will overcome these difficulties. Just as men see in a single universal church a solution which is destined to banish all creedal differences and end sectarian strifes and denominational disputes, so in the political world, it is supposed, strife will be eliminated by casting all nations into one political mold and erecting a world empire. The objections cited against the former group also hold, in substance, against this group. These also ignore the fact of sin. They forget that a world empire—unless all people would think alike, a thing which is impossible to the end of time in a sinful world such as ours—would imply oppression and persecution to large numbers and itself create bitterness, a greater grief than that which it would remove. World empires in the past have only been able to maintain themselves by sheer force and were generally short-lived; and the lesson of history would teach us that they are destined to be so in the future.

Parallel to this spirit of internationalism, there is rampant in the world today a strong and equally assertive spirit of nationalism. The spirit of the French Revolution with its paganistic humanism and exaltation of the individual at the expense of the community underlies much of this nationalism. It glorifies the state as the highest expression of all that is great and mighty in the individual man. The state becomes the apotheosis, the exaltation, of the individual ego. Each nation consequently considers its type of culture better than any other. There is then no peaceful living next to the other nations with a distinct culture; but each considers itself and its own culture the best, and regards its own highest destiny and calling to be to strive to be king of the universe. It has no higher ambition than to foist its own peculiar culture upon other nations, either by peaceful means or by war. Such nationalism—or imperialism—is death to all harmony and unity in the family of nations and a fruitful breeding ground for imperialistic wars. This spirit is obvious in such nationalistic countries as present-day

Russia. But that spirit is not absent in other lands, including America.

We can readily see that, as Calvinists, we cannot agree with a one-sided internationalism or with a one-sided nationalism. Just as in the church, Calvinism has been opposed to a one-sided individualism as strongly as to a one-sided collectivism, and, likewise, in the regulation of the internal affairs of the state, so the same general fact meets us here. We cannot endorse either a nationalism or an internationalism which ignores either the one or the other of these principles. Both are needed for a proper development of the cultural life of the world today. Not a world empire in which the distinct nations are eliminated, but a family of nations in which each is free to develop its own cultural task, and in which all these distinct nations are properly correlated and regulated by international law, is the ideal for which we should strive. How this ideal is to be approximated, and the difficulties it encounters, we hope to indicate in the next chapter.

18

Internationalism and the United Nations

In the face of the acute problem raised by the thought of internationalism and the variety of opinions which are held, what stand should a Calvinistic Christian take? It certainly would be unwise, without any definite guiding principles, to allow these weighty international problems to be settled by the impulses of the moment, or by what seems to be advisable in a given instance, or by whatever convenience may dictate. In the end such a shortsighted policy would prove ruinous to institutions which we hold most dear. What we need are definite and sound principles. The Bible, which is our rule for faith and practice in all domains of life, should be our guide also in the determination of these principles.

The Calvinist and International Relations

If we investigate what Calvinism has done in this field in the past, we shall not be altogether disappointed. It is true that leading men in the field of politics in the nineteenth century, like Groen Van Prinsterer and Abraham Kuyper, have not left us much material on international relations. The problems of internationalism were in their day not as acute as today, and internal affairs demanded much more of their attention. However, what they did say, does suggest the principles, though not extensively developed. During Kuyper's day we had an important study by D. P. D. Fabius entitled *Volkenrecht,* which is full of valuable information.[1] In more recent times men like Hendrik Colyn and W. H. Rutgers devoted much attention to these problems and have labored together with the League of Nations and other important movements to help solve them.

It would, however, be a mistake to suppose that Calvinism had nothing to say about internationalism prior to the time of these Calvinistic leaders. John Calvin concerned himself with the biblical principles which should govern states in their international relations. Calvin—occupied as he was with the wars of religion—had much to say about such international affairs as peaceful diplomacy, the right of intervention by war, and the problem of war. The modern humanitarian and ethical movement against war, insofar as it seeks to substitute a system of covenants between nations and courts of arbitration for war wherever possible, will find much valuable material in Calvin's writings. Also the French Calvinists, like Mornay in his *Vindiciae contra tyrannos* (1574), have given valuable food for thought on principles of internationalism.

If we examine the Bible in search of the principles to which these and other Calvinists refer, there are many individual texts which could be cited with profit. Far more valuable information, however, will be gained from a study of basic views which underlie the whole of Scripture, insofar as these bear upon the question of internationalism.

There is first of all the scriptural view that God "made out of one every nation of men to dwell on all the face of the earth" (Acts 17:26). God did not create several independent human races or nations. He created one human pair from whom arose all the nations of the earth. All men as creatures are, therefore, brothers, related to one another by ties of blood and common creaturely origin. Furthermore, the Creator gave that one human race a single set of laws which should govern them in their manifold relationships. Legally and morally the several nations and peoples have a common law, the law of God, which binds them together and should determine their relationships. On the basis of this common law there are general ethical principles which should be considered settled and binding for the nations. On the Christian basis there is, therefore, definitely such a thing as international law, which is obligatory for all nations.

Although all nations form a racial unity, there is also, according to Scripture, a definite place for such natural group formations as distinct nations. This important fact must not be overlooked. Had the human race remained sinless, there would have arisen in the organic life of men larger and lesser groups, each with its own cultural task and sovereignty in its own sphere commensurate with the task assigned to it. Sin, which has disrupted human life generally, has also worked havoc with the cultural demand of God to each of these groups, that they subdue the earth and accomplish the special task assigned to each of them. Instead of the unity which God had intended that organic groups should attain through diversity, each developing its own distinctive task, there arose an attempt at uniformity without distinctiveness. The classic biblical example of such godless uniformity is given us in the story of the erection of the tower of Babel on the plains of Shinar. Had this project been executed, there would have arisen a godless world empire, in which the subjugation of the earth and the development of the diversified talents of men and cultural tasks generally would have been retarded greatly, not to say defeated.[2]

When God came down from heaven to break up this uniformity by the so-called confusion of tongues, we must not understand what happened there to have been a mere change in language, with a Babylonish jargon as the only result. That is too childish and simple a view of the matter. The difference in language at Babel, as it always is between peoples of differing tongues, is only an indication of distinct characteristics and inclinations which are peculiar to the different peoples. What God did was to change their preferred habits and tastes, as well as speech, so that these men no longer desired to live together. They were now living in distinct worlds of thought. Hence one went out in one direction, another in another. This fact is clearly indicated by the genealogies of Genesis 10 and 11, which describe the period immediately following the history of Babel's tower. These genealogies also seem to indicate that the confusion of tongues did not extend to each separate individual but to the groups of individuals represented by the various families. Had the difference created by the confusion of tongues been merely a divergence in language and nothing more, within a short time that difficulty might have been overcome. Now the families preferred to live apart.

These juxtaposed characteristics witnessed at Babel are also the outstanding contrasts in distinct nations. We notice not only a difference in language, but an unlikeness in aptitudes, tastes, and dominant characteristics which leads each to interest itself in a distinct line of thought and cultural activity. There are, therefore, two basic factors inherent in the very nature of things which affect the way in which the several peoples of the earth should live together in their international relations. The unity of the human race obliges them to live together as members of one family, but the distinct characteristics, the tastes and cultural tasks of the several nations and peoples, call for a corresponding independence and sovereignty in their own spheres. This their God-given cultural duties demand. A single world empire stresses uniformity at the expense of diversity. This sort of world we will have with us when the Antichrist aspires to power. He will force all parts of his realm to conform to a single standard in religion, politics, and business, without allowing room for the proper development of diversity of gifts. And nationalism, which exalts its own nation and will hear of no responsibilities to other nations except insofar as it may choose for its own selfish interests to make compacts and agreements, stresses diversity at the precious cost of international unity. The Calvinist believes that in a sinless world there would have been a normal development of both racial unity and the diversity of its several parts, each group applying itself to its own cultural task while at the same time cooperating harmoniously with every other part for the realization of the cultural ideal set for humanity as a whole by the Creator. This ideal in a sinless world will once again be realized in the glorious kingdom of God established through the redemptive work of Jesus Christ. The Calvinist also believes that in this world of sin, for the good order of the human race, God in his common grace has made provision for the government of the world by law, whereby is recognized both the common tie that binds all men together in a family of nations and the distinct characteristics and cultural tasks which the several national groups have independently. Consequently, the Calvinist stands committed to the type of internationalism which is in a general way expressed by the term "United Nations."

The Calvinist and the United Nations

From this we can learn what the Calvinist will think of the existing United Nations. If that organization really aims to be, as its name implies, a union of nations in which each retains its own national sovereignty necessary for the dispatch of its own cultural duty, while each at the same time assumes a conscious responsibility for its part in the tasks common to the family of nations, then the United Nations embodies a genuine scriptural ideal and demands our appreciation and support. Should it over the course of time develop into another godless superstate as at Babel, where the divine command given to the distinct nations is ignored, than the union would not foster much hope or deserve our support. The United Nations as a melting pot of peoples in which God-ordained distinctions tend to be eradicated by the erection of a uniform world empire is a thing to be feared rather than desired.

The duty of the Christian toward the United Nations in its present state seems thereby indicated. In the present formation of the United Nations there are good elements and bad, ideas which the Christian can laud and others which he must condemn. International relations generally as they exist today are a composite of Roman, Greek, Egyptian, Christian, Marxist, and other elements. The Christian, in his duty to be a leavening influence, should exert himself to the utmost to promote whatever is good in the United Nations as he would in any national affairs, and to seek to make it conform increasingly to the principles laid down in God's Word. He will recognize that it will ever be a more hopeful and helpful agent for the well being of humanity in the measure that its members succeed in making it conform to the principles of the sacred Word. We should not hold ourselves aloof, but with proper reservations should seek to promote its interests.

The argument that the Untied Nations may in time become an instrument of false ideals, or even a stepping-stone for the kingdom of the Antichrist, should not restrain us from lending it in its present state our support, and from endeavoring to make of it a powerful instrument for the promotion of better international relations. If we refuse to support it because of a possible abuse of authority, we might also, on the same basis, object to the support of any church or civil government.

Churches especially have been known, after a season of blessing, to have passed over into wrong hands and thereby become instruments of evil. The history of more than one great orthodox denomination, which has rendered yeoman service at one period in its history but later turned liberal, is living witness of that fact. When the time of such defection in an international league has come, it will become the duty of the Christian to withdraw, but not before.

A careful scrutiny of the charter of the United Nations, the decisions of its Security Council, and its current activities in world affairs would seem to demand our devoted support at the present time. It is, indeed, regrettable that the United Nations, under the pressure of atheistic Russia, has refused to recognize the sovereignty of God, but the organization does recognize many values the Calvinist cherishes. It believes in the independence of national units within responsible limits; it has consistently opposed unjust aggression; it has championed international law against banditry. It is thus our duty to support the United Nations until it clearly becomes an influence for evil instead of good.

19

International Law

The Calvinist favors the kind of relation between nations which is indicated by the term "United Nations." He is not in favor of a uniform world empire in which all nations are compelled to conform to a single standard of living and the characteristic national distinctions tend to be wiped out. Nor does he favor the idea of absolutely distinct nations, between which there is no firm bond uniting them.

The Need of a World Court

Such a union of nations will require a central governing body, some world court where the affairs of the union can be administered. Such a central body may act in a purely advisory capacity, be a mere court of arbitration, or it may be vested with a certain measure of legislative, executive, and judicial power, intended to make its decisions binding. The trend in the United Nations has been to clothe it with such mandatory powers, rather than to leave the execution of its decisions to the nations within the league. The League of Nations at Geneva decided to use compulsory measures to make its decrees effective, such as economic boycotts, and at one time even determined upon a military force which would have the right to compel obedience to its decisions, in the event that any member nation would violate them and thereby jeopardize the rights and well being of the nations within the League. We know that when the time came to apply these decisions, the

League hesitated to do so because of dissension in its ranks. But the fact that the League so decided at least indicates the stand to which it had come, which it felt it must of necessity take.

Calvinism and a World Court

In such a world court clothed with mandatory powers there is always the danger that it may develop too much power and become a superstate. This is especially true today, since the trend is in the direction of consolidation of nations and the formation of world empires. Nevertheless, from the Calvinistic point of view there can be no objection as a matter of principle to clothing such a world court with limited powers. The federal government of the United States has received a measure of federal power delegated to it by the member states which form the Union. This idea of a federal government clothed with mandatory powers has always been considered to be in perfect harmony with the views of Calvinism, as long as the rights of the states of the Union received adequate protection. Thus also a federal government of a United States of the world, it would seem, would be in full accord with Calvinistic principles and ideals, as long as the rights of the member states would receive adequate guarantee and protection.

Article 18, inserted in the Program of Principles of the Anti-Revolutionary party of the Netherlands in 1934, is illuminating in that it indicates the views on internationalism held by the Dutch Calvinists. It reads:

> For the relations with other nations it [i.e., the Anti-Revolutionary party] teaches, that also these are governed by the ordinances, which God has instituted over the nations; with the understanding that, with undiminished maintenance of their own national independence, energetic co-operation is required for the development of the right of federation of nations and thereby of the peaceable settlement of disputes between nations, as well as counteracting, if necessary with armed force, of all unrighteous exercise of force, and for the development of a society and co-operation of nations, which corresponds to law and justice, and promotes the spiritual and material interests of the people.

The Basis of International Law

A question of primary importance is the one which inquires into the ultimate ground on which international law rests. Is the ground of authority in international affairs only and ultimately the sovereign will of the separate nations which enter into international relations? Is every nation autonomous, a law unto itself, so that it can decide what it will, as long as it has sufficient force to defend its actions? If so, then with the same sort of logic, we must conclude that no nation need join the United Nations if it does not so choose. Then it does not need to concern itself about other nations, or when once a member, it is only bound by the force of its own agreements which it has entered into voluntarily. And since there is no authority beyond its own decisions, it can terminate these agreements at will, whenever its own selfish interests so dictate; for there is no superior power to which it is answerable. Upon such a basis there is, strictly speaking, no such thing as international law; there are merely international agreements, treaties, and compacts, which depend for their validity solely upon the arbitrary will of the contracting nations.

We may therefore ask: Is there any such thing as international law, and if so, what is the ground on which this international law rests? Many diverse opinions have been advanced on this subject. In general it can be said that, prior to the middle of the eighteenth century, it was a common, even though not a universal opinion, that there were three sources of international law. First of all, there were general principles of law, independent of the will of any government yet having binding effect upon all. Next, there was the law of universal custom. Certain customs were reckoned to have become established usages and hence had the validity of law for universal observance. Besides these, as a third source, statutory regulations which nations had mutually agreed to observe were considered to have binding force for all.

Beginning about the middle of the eighteenth century and throughout the nineteenth century, an opinion, which had already been sounded by Machiavelli in the early fifteenth century, grew to be paramount. In this the validity of general principles of justice was denied. It made the state, or the sovereign people, or the ruler the court of last resort. Nothing could bind nations except their own will.

It is evident that such ideas of international relations lead to international anarchy. On this basis treaties can be made and arbitrarily broken, as the convenience of any nation may dictate. International chaos will be, as it in great measure currently is, the result. This condition has led in recent years to a growing sense of the need for international laws and principles which exist independently of and above the individual nations, to the observance of which the nations will consider themselves in conscience bound.

The great problem lies in ascertaining the ground on which such laws and principles must rest. The positivist maintains that there are no binding principles behind the laws which men or nations may choose to make; at best, there are only underlying customs. However, as can readily be seen, customs need not be binding on any man's or nation's conscience. The pragmatist, on the other hand, would insist that laws of nations are binding because practical utility so dictates. From this it would follow, however, that if practical advantage would dictate something very different, or the very opposite, there is nothing to prevent a change. All guarantee that laws will be observed is thereby lost.

The instability of such grounds has led a growing number today to revert to the theory of natural law which was prevalent two or more centuries ago. According to this theory there lies behind all positive laws which nations make a common law which holds for all, which is inherent in nature itself. Of this "law of nature" human reason and conscience are adjudged to be the interpreters. There is something attractive about this theory, even though it has been tried in history and found wanting. Here at least we have an objective norm, which is outside of men and does not change as do such subjective regulations as those which custom, or practical utility, or the uncertain opinion of rulers or people may dictate. The objection, however, lies not so much in the law of nature itself. The Creator has endowed all men with certain inalienable laws. But the difficulty lies in making reason and conscience its interpreters. For from this it follows, as historically has been the case, that a wide variety of conflicting opinions would result. No one then knows just what the law of nature really demands.

The only recourse seems to be the adoption of the Christian position, which finds in the will of God as interpreted in the

Bible the objective norm on which all law must rest. Here we find objective eternal principles, free from subjective coloring, and, as God's law, binding upon every man's conscience.

Against the objection that such law would only hold for converted Christians and hence would be inapplicable in a world such as ours, the Christian would suggest a threefold reply. For the Christian himself there can be no other ultimate ground on which human laws must rest than the will of God, of which the Bible is the interpreter. And he may never yield the point that a man or nation is relieved of recognizing the sovereignty of God or the authority of his Word in case either chooses not to believe. The Christians of the first century, following the leadership of the apostles in this, notably Paul, never conceded that point. They rather demanded that all men and nations come to the acknowledgment of it. And it is the Christian's duty as a leaven in human society to develop this consciousness among men. Furthermore, it is not a fact that the Christian view of the sovereignty of God and regard for the Bible as norm will not succeed with non-Christians and is therefore inapplicable in a world such as ours. No view has universal approbation. Hence, reasoning on such basis no view would work. But it is a fact of history, repeatedly illustrated, that the more Christians propagated their views and insisted on the observance of Christian ideals, the more consciences of people in general became Christianized, and the greater was the conformity to these ideals. In practice there is no alternative that will work; although men have racked their brains, they have not discovered any. If people no longer have respect for God's law or for the Bible, and if truth and righteousness have no firmer grounding than the customs of people or practical utility, there is nothing but force that, in the end, will stop them in striving for the attainment of their own selfish ends. Then let us build ever greater armies and navies, and let there be a mad rush for ever bigger armaments, and heaven only knows to what that will lead. In order to be effective morals must have their basis in religion, in the consciousness of the sovereignty of God, or even morality among nations becomes a failure. The words of Scripture seem to have a direct bearing here: "To the law and to the testimony! If they speak not according to this word, surely there is no morning for them" (Isa. 8:20).

The Concerns of International Law

Which matters fall within the domain of a world court or union of nations? In the main it can be said that a parallel can be drawn here between the duties of such a world court and the duties of a federal government like that of the United States as discussed in previous chapters. As in the case of the U.S. government, in a federation of nations these duties will lie in a twofold direction; namely, the administration of international justice between the several nations and the promotion of the general welfare, or the dispatch of those cultural duties which nations cannot effect working independently. On the other hand, whatever belongs strictly to the domain of the nations separately, or to distinct cultural groups in society, will not fall within its scope. The rule which is to guide the federal government in its relation to the states of the union or to social groups within its domain also would seem to hold true here, that the initiative of the several nations and groups in human society shall have the priority over the actions of the world court. Whatever can successfully be performed by the nations themselves shall not be a matter of concern to the world court. It must never seek to take over these distinct tasks of the independent nations, but it must rather foster their self-activity.

In the administration of international law, we can distinguish between laws which relate to the rights and duties of private citizens of a country in foreign lands and those which relate to nations as a whole in their relations to each other. The rights of individuals on foreign soil, both as these concern their life and their property, must be determined and protected by laws which nations agree to observe.

Not only the interests of private citizens but also the public interests of nations as a whole in their relations to each other must be safeguarded by international law. These public rights should not be restricted to such legal rights as have once been established by law, but they concern moral rights as well. Nations, as well as individuals, have moral obligations to each other which they may not ignore. A moral principle of general nature which should be observed by all, applicable to numerous cases, is the law of love, which is well circumscribed in the words of Christ: "Whatsoever ye would that men should do to you, do ye even so to them" (Matt. 7:12).

A specific application of this moral principle concerns the problem of intervention and nonintervention. May and should a state intervene in the affairs of another state when basic human interests, such as religious liberty, or the possession of life and property, are jeopardized? Many have answered this question in the negative and have maintained a policy of strict nonintervention. While from a practical point of view such policy may seem expedient because it enables a nation to escape difficulties for itself, from the Christian point of view a policy of absolute nonintervention stands condemned. God has made of one blood all nations of the earth, and they together form one family. We may not excuse ourselves from the obligation of intervention when basic rights are trampled on by tyrannous governments by adopting the attitude of Cain: "Am I my brother's keeper?" In practice the policy of nonintervention has never been strictly observed. Our own Monroe Doctrine, while it denies intervention of European powers in American affairs, nevertheless acknowledges a certain right of intervention by the United States in the affairs of other nations on this continent.

It may be difficult to determine in each instance just when intervention is demanded. At times intervention will do more harm than good. Each case will have to be determined by its own exigencies. Often, too, nations have intervened because of unworthy motives. But the fact remains that love for our neighbor demands in certain instances intervention in the affairs of foreign nations as well as in the affairs of other families. A private family's rights are in normal circumstances inviolable as well as those of nations. But when the rights of members of the family are jeopardized, it may become such a serious matter that other families may have to intervene. So, too, when the vital interests of citizens of any nation which is neighbor to us are endangered, their religious convictions trampled upon, or their very life threatened, it will be our duty to intervene and help establish proper order, either by peaceful means, or even if necessary by coercion. William the Silent intervened in the war of Spain with its Dutch colonies on the ground that, as prince of Orange, an independent principality, he was free. When he saw that the citizens of Holland were subjected to religious and political tyranny, he felt it his Christian duty to intervene.

The specific rights which each nation may claim of every

other nation can be conveniently grouped under the following three heads. First of all, each nation has the right of self-preservation and independence. As long as it does not infringe upon the rights of other nations, no nation may rob it of its territory or due rights. This involves the privilege of self-defense, the maintenance of military and naval power, and a line of defense necessary for such self-preservation. It also has the right of self-development. This involves such matters of international interest as colonization, trade relations, exports and imports, tariffs, and promotion of its agricultural, commercial, and industrial interests. As a third right, it may claim national respect, through proper treatment accorded its envoys and other representatives, flag, and national emblems by other countries.

For the promotion of this threefold right which each nation may claim, there arises the necessity of diplomatic relations between the nations, with the establishment of embassies and consulates in foreign countries through which such rights and duties may be regulated. For the same reason also, nations must of necessity make treaties, form alliances, and enter into covenants, because there is no superstate that can with sovereign power impose these international regulations upon the individual nations. The value of United Nations with a court where general rules governing such international relations are agreed upon can readily be seen. The more specifically agreements between any nations conform to general standards of international justice, the better in the long run will be the condition of all concerned.

When peaceful diplomacy fails to maintain proper relations between nations, the recourse of an offended nation is to the use of armed force to defend its rights and privileges. This fact leads us to the discussion of the moot problem of war.

20

War in History

War is one of the most dreadful evils that can happen to any people. It not only involves much destruction of property and of life; but it leaves in its wake a trail of poverty, of widowhood and orphanage, and it retards the progress of much that is good and desirable for the advancement of civilization.[1]

The Origin of War

War is almost as old as the human race. Almost, but not entirely. To be specific, it is as old as sin. Since the entrance of sin into the world, two things have happened which account for war. The one is the presence of two opposing forces in this world, the force of righteousness and the force of iniquity, God and the devil. These two forces can never live together in harmony. A continuous conflict will rage between them until one is completely subdued. For this reason, already, war is bound to exist in this present world between God and the devil, between the archangel Michael with the holy angels and the devil and his angels, between God's people and the proponents of unrighteousness, as the history of divine revelation reveals. The other cause of war brought about by the entrance of sin is the demoralizing influence of sin upon human life itself, causing hatred and selfishness and strife not only between individuals, but between groups of individuals and nations as a whole. We can, therefore, expect periodic outbursts of war as long as sin and its virus is with us, even though much can be done in

God's common grace to check such outbursts and make possible a measure of peace and civilization.

Christianity, Martial Spirits, and Pacifists

Men have differed sharply in their attitudes toward war: some have glorified it as manly and heroic; others have regarded it as satanic and wholly evil. No sharp line of demarcation can here be drawn between non-Christians and Christians. Martial spirits and pacifists have been found among both the pagan peoples of antiquity and early Christians, and are still found in the ranks of non-Christians and Christians today. To mention but a few of the outstanding contenders for either view, men like Heraclitus, Machiavelli, Vattel, Hegel, and Nietzsche have all advanced theories which eulogized war; whereas men like Tolstoi, Kirby Page, and Harry Emerson Fosdick have been absolute pacifists, outlawing all war.

The most prominent militarists in a country have not always been those who were engaged in warfare as a livelihood. For, in the nineteenth century, to cite but one illustration, certain philosophers did more to foment war than leaders of the army. Among the Christians of the early centuries of Christianity there were many who opposed war, not as a matter of principle, but because it required their entering into the service of a government which persecuted Christians and demanded worship of idols by the militia. When the Roman eagle was exchanged for the cross and the empire turned Christian, the attitude toward war among the Christians underwent a corresponding change. The later outstanding leaders of the church, whose views have been dominant in Christendom, like Ambrosius, Augustine, Thomas Aquinas, Luther, and Calvin, sided neither with the out-and-out militarists nor with the out-and-out pacifists, but justified a limited use of war in certain cases and with definite restrictions.

One's View of Life and One's View of War

While defenders and opponents of war are found among all classes and in all periods of history, it is nevertheless true that one's attitude to war is in the main determined by the view of life to which he is committed. A few examples will illustrate this point. Hegel begins his philosophy with the idea that the world is an unbroken process of development of the absolute idea. In the state, which unites in itself the family and society, which is the most complete realization of liberty and morality and in fact the loftiest organization known to man and should consequently be worshiped, he finds the highest organization of this idea among men. The state exercises force to realize the idea which it embodies and should exercise it. War is a necessary means of the state for its self-realization and should, therefore, be exalted as a worthy institution. Views like those of Hegel have been reflected in the policies of Bismarck and others, and have done much to foment war.

On the other hand, views of materialistic evolutionists, like those of Darwin and Haeckel, have led many to an antithetical conclusion. Man was thought to have evolved from the brute state, in which war was a natural mode of existence. As man emerges and civilization advances, wars will increasingly diminish until finally men will have outgrown their brute instincts altogether and wars will be a thing of the past. Among the advocates of a universal, uniform world empire in which all national distinctions are eliminated, and among pacifists, there are many who hold this viewpoint.

On a Christian basis absolute pacifism has been defended by the Anabaptists of the sixteenth and seventeenth centuries. Most Anabaptists did not deny that governments were needed in a sinful world and that these governments must at times use force and wage warfare. But the civil government belonged to the sphere of "the world," which was entirely distinct from the church. He who was a follower of Christ belonged to a different sphere. He might not use force or wage warfare, take an oath of allegiance to the civil government, or enter into the service of the state. Some Anabaptists further even went and rejected all civil governments and all political magistrates in Christian countries. These might be good and proper in heathen lands and among unconverted peoples, but once a nation became Christianized, political governments must vanish. In any event the Christian should not participate in civic affairs. The political revolt of Münster is an example of the more extreme Anabaptist position on this point.

The attitude of the Anabaptist follows directly from the theological views entertained in this circle. Although there was a wide divergence of opinion among them on several points, a prevalent view was that Christ in his redemptive work does not save the social order of existing humanity. The present human race, and with it the social order, is doomed to destruction. Christ himself did not enter this human race by taking upon himself the flesh and blood of Mary. He took with him a human body from heaven which passed through his mother and so began an entirely new humanity. All Christians at regeneration receive an entirely new creation which has nothing to do with and is entirely distinct from their old selves and, therefore, also entirely distinct from the present social order of humanity. The church, therefore, has nothing to do with the present social or political order, except to rescue men from it by evangelical and missionary activity. All efforts to influence this present world to the good by scientific or educational means, and all attempts to permeate it as a leaven in society are futile. It is dead and will remain dead. On such a basis absolute pacifism is a logical conclusion.

This Anabaptist position might not be of such vital interest to us of the present day were it not for the fact that in the fundamentalist camp many have adopted a position which is in whole or in part akin to this Anabaptist view, and have maintained essentially the same attitude toward political, social, and educational affairs, specifically toward the problem of war. This is especially true of many of the millennialists, whose hopes for reformation of society are wholly pinned upon the premillennial return of Christ to earth when he will set up his millennial kingdom. Efforts to exert a leavening influence upon educational, social, or political life are considered futile. Christianity has but one duty to society, and that is to win converts to Christianity by missionary effort. The consciousness that the Christian is part and parcel of state and society and has a present duty in it remains undeveloped. There is an apathy toward the settlement of international problems, either by peacetime or by wartime methods. Instead of this, a spirit of aloofness, or asceticism, is studiously cultivated. It is unfortunate that at the present time the religious pendulum of the great American public swings almost entirely between modernism and millennial fundamentalism, ignoring other important types of Christianity like Calvinism and Lutheranism.

The modernist differs from the fundamentalist in making the social and political aspects of Christianity his main interest. He expects to bring about reform in human society, not by any supernatural influences of Christ or by the consecrated efforts of Christians, but upon a purely naturalistic basis by powers which are native to man. With a naturalistic and largely evolutionary basis, many modernists are obsessed with a utopian ideal of a future warless world. The spirit of pacifism—often absolute pacifism, as in the case of Fosdick—is favored by them but on a very different basis than that of the fundamentalists.

Revived Interest in the Problem of War

Since the opening of the twentieth century, the problem of war has come to the foreground and has commanded widespread attention for a very natural reason. After the nineteenth century—the great age of invention, particularly in the realm of steam and electricity—the nations of the earth have been brought into much closer relationship than in former ages. The inhabitants of Europe and even of the Orient are our neighbors today. What happens in the Far East now is known to us the same day. This proximity of the different nations and peoples has by no means made for a united human race. While the proximity of the different peoples has promoted an increased resemblance in superficial matters, such as habits of dress, it has tended to intensify basic differences. The clash of basic ideals and interests has become a fruitful source of war between the nations. The rising conflicts between those who are committed to democratic ideals and those who are committed to totalitarian ideals is a pertinent example. Facts of this type have prompted men to give much closer study to the possibilities of averting war, of curbing its evils, and of promoting peace among nations. Ever since the first Hague Conference of 1899, many peace movements have been organized, both in the form of unofficial pacifist conferences and official peace congresses of nations.[2]

In the face of widespread differences of opinion on the problem of war, and of the acute interest which has in recent years been awakened in it because of the complex nature of contemporary society, what should be the attitude of the Calvinist? This we shall determine next as we study what our sourcebook, the Bible, has to say on this matter.

21

The Bible and War

As we approach the Bible to discover the principles which are to govern our attitude toward war, we are immediately confronted with the dilemma that among the many scriptural texts relating to war are some which favor it and others which just as emphatically oppose it. It is small wonder that the Bible has been appealed to by all parties, by militarists and pacifists alike. Each found in it an array of texts which seemed to favor his chosen position. A few passages taken almost at random will illustrate this point. "The Lord is a man of war" (Exod. 15:3); "He maketh wars to cease unto the end of the earth" (Ps. 46:9); "Thou shalt not kill" (Exod. 20:13); "Go, and utterly destroy the sinners, the Amalekites, and fight against them until they be consumed" (1 Sam. 15:18); "He teacheth my hands to war" (2 Sam. 22:35); "Thou shalt not build an house for my name, because thou hast been a man of war, and hast shed blood" (1 Chron. 28:3); "Blessed are the peacemakers, for they shall be called the children of God" (Matt. 5:9); "The Lord our God . . . hath avenged the blood of his servants at her hand" (Rev. 19:2); "Avenge not yourselves, but rather give place unto wrath" (Rom. 12:19); "For he [i.e., the government] beareth not the sword in vain, for he is a minister of God, a revenger to execute wrath" (Rom. 13:4); "From whence come wars and fightings among you, come they not hence, even of your lusts that war in your members? Ye lust and have not, ye kill and desire to have, and cannot obtain, ye fight and war, yet ye have not, because ye ask not" (James 4:1, 2); "In righteousness he doth judge and make war" (Rev. 19:11).

The problem which such seemingly contradictory passages present cannot be solved by the suggestion that the Bible does contain conflicting statements. It is true that there are so-called paradoxical statements in the Bible, statements which seem to be logical opposites, as God's sovereignty and human responsibility, or God's transcendence and his immanence, facts too profound for the mind of man to comprehend. But there are no actual contradictions in the Bible. To us as Reformed people the Bible presents one consistent view of divine revelation. We believe that the divine Author of God's Word would not contradict in one place what he said in another.

Nor can we extricate ourselves from the dilemma by maintaining that Old Testament ethics permitted war, but New Testament ethics does not. For, according to Reformed belief, there is only one consistent view of ethics in the whole Bible. Nor will it aid us to assert that there are many battles recorded in the Bible, particularly in the Old Testament, but without divine approval, and that they are not intended as a rule for our lives. It is claimed that these battles are simply recorded, without reference to their justifiability. We discover, however, that several of the wars mentioned in the Old Testament were waged at the express command of Jehovah. Certainly God would not command something which is sinful. Nor can we solve the problem by maintaining that God permitted wars in Old Testament times just as he allowed divorce, because of the low level of the people, for we know that several of the wars of Israel were not permissive wars but campaigns carried on at the express will of Jehovah.

We cannot solve our problem, moreover, by maintaining that the New Testament expressly forbids war. For no such statement can be found in the New Testament. On the contrary, just where we might expect to find such a prohibition in the New Testament, it is omitted. When the soldiers come to John the Baptist, asking "What must we do?" he does not demand of them withdrawal from the army, but requires a moral act: "Do violence to no man, neither accuse any falsely, and be content with your wages" (Luke 3:14). Paul never required his soldier friends to leave the army. And the centurion Cornelius, although employed in the Roman army, is spoken of as a devout man and acceptable to God (Acts 10:1–6).

The Two Spheres

How then must these apparent conflicts be explained? We have only to examine the specific sphere to which each of these texts applies to solve the basic difficulty. It all depends upon whether the passage in question refers to private individuals in their relationships within the kingdom of God or to public officials in their responsibilities to the civil state. An example or two taken from the passages cited above will illustrate the point. The text taken from Exodus 20:13, "Thou shalt not kill," forbids all murder. Nevertheless the same law commands the government to put to death the Sabbath-breaker and other violators of the moral code and to wage war against the enemies of Israel, for example, Amalek. In Romans 12:19, Christians as private individuals are told not to avenge themselves; but in the very next chapter, six verses later we are told that the civil government is "the minister of God, a revenger to execute wrath upon him that doeth evil" (Rom. 13:4).

The Sermon on the Mount is a favorite portion of Scripture referred to as evidence that it is wrong for a Christian to wage war. In it Jesus is describing to the multitude the proper conduct within the kingdom of God. He very definitely preaches the doctrine of nonresistance (cf. Matt. 5:5, 9, 10, 21, 38–42, 43–45). But if these sayings of Jesus were to be understood as applying to the conduct of civil governments, they would prove far too much. For in that same Sermon on the Mount we are urged to nonresistance in the following terms: "If any man will sue thee at the law, and take away thy coat, let him have thy cloak also" (Matt. 5:40). That very demand of nonresistance would then forbid us to have civil courts of justice, including even the World Court, of which the pacifist is an ardent defender.

There is only one text of those frequently referred to in defense of absolute pacifism to which the distinction between conduct of private citizens in the kingdom of God and duties of the civil state does not apply: 1 Chronicles 28:3, in which David is denied the privilege of building the temple because he has been a man of war and has shed blood. That text cannot properly be interpreted to imply a condemnation of all war. For it would be strange indeed if David would first be commended for carrying on the wars of Jehovah, and later be penalized for doing what the Lord had repeatedly and expressly instructed him to do. The reason for the prohibition to build the temple is obviously another. The temple has reference directly to the spiritual relations of men in the kingdom of God, which is a kingdom of peace. Such a kingdom can only be properly symbolized by a king of peace as its builder, not by a man of war as David was, even though his wars were wars of Jehovah.

The fact that the Bible draws a clear distinction between necessary conduct within the kingdom of God and duties of the civil state does not, however, explain why such distinctions must be drawn. The kingdom of God in its internal organization and relations is a kingdom of righteousness and joy and peace. Its citizens, as members of that kingdom, are children of righteousness and peace, and should in their private relations overcome evil with good and force by nonresistance. A Christian, in his private life, should not avenge himself, or "stand on his own rights," but willingly yield "his rights," wherever reasonably possible, even toward non-Christians, and thus win over the adversary or put him to shame. Such a pacifistic spirit if applied by Christians in Christian lands will do a world of good, not only in reducing personal strifes, but in allaying the war spirit between nations.

The determinative question, however, in the settlement of the problem of war is whether, in a sinful world, justice can be maintained without the use of force. Were all injustice in this world to be met by nonresistance only, those who would be motivated by greed and selfishness and lust would soon have the upper hand; and life, liberty, and the pursuit of happiness in an orderly society would become an impossibility. There comes a time, when, after peaceable attempts at settlement of disputes have failed, the only recourse is to the use of force to stop iniquity in its onward march. When appeals to conscience, righteousness, and truth fail, the only way to stop brute force is by force. Even God Almighty employs force to check evil-doing men and evil-doing nations after they have spurned his appeals to practice righteousness. And Jesus Christ, at the end of this dispensation of grace, will employ no other means than force to overcome wickedness, for we read: "But those mine enemies, which would not that I should reign over them, bring hither and slay them before me" (Luke 19:27). God repeatedly has directed nations to use force for the suppression of evil, either within the nations themselves or in other nations. Think, for example, of the instruction to Israel to destroy the Canaanitish nations and the use of Assyria and Babylon to punish degenerate Israel.

However, God does not entrust the maintenance of justice by force in this world to private individuals but to the civil government. To Christians who in their private relations would live as citizens of the kingdom of God all such injunctions apply as, "Avenge not yourselves," "give place to wrath," and the like. But the civil government has as its special task the administration of justice and must see to it that this world is not overrun by evil. The same Bible which in Romans 12:19–21 demands nonresistance of private individuals, in Romans 13:1–6 informs us that the government is a "minister of God to thee for good," and is "an avenger for wrath to him that doeth evil," and for this purpose bears the sword. The Belgic Confession gives us the Reformed point of view on this matter when it states (art. 36) that the civil government is instituted by God "to the end that the dissoluteness of men might be restrained, and all things carried on among them with good order and decency. For this purpose He has invested the magistracy with the sword for the punishment of evildoers and for the protection of them that do well." Now, whether these evildoers be only one or a few which can be put down by police force, or whether they are so numerous as to require a whole army and navy does not alter the principle involved. It is the specific task of the government to restrain evil by force, of which the sword is the symbol.

Calvin states the matter thus; "It is the dictate both of natural equity, and of the nature of the office, therefore, that princes are armed, not only to restrain the crimes of private individuals by judicial punishments, but also to defend the territories committed to their charge by going to war against any hostile aggression; and the Holy Spirit, in many passages of Scripture, declares such wars to be lawful."[1]

It might be argued that Paul in Romans 13:1–6 is not speaking of war between nations since the context indicates that the reference is to the relation of the government to its own citizens, not to other governments. But even if the duty of governments to wield the sword would be limited strictly to its internal affairs, the text would not outlaw all war but tacitly admit the justifiability of certain wars. For there is also civil war and internal revolution, of which our own Civil War is an example. In such cases surely the cry of the pacifists of Civil War times does not hold: "If you take a sword and dror it, And go stick a feller through, Government ain't to answer for it, God will send the bill to you." Most assuredly government is to answer for it since to it, and not to men as private individuals, is the task assigned to execute vengeance upon evil, for which task it is given the sword. And if the government already has the right and the duty to wage war against rebellious subjects within its borders, it is hard to see why, for the same moral reason, the government is not appointed by God to defend the inhabitants of its own country when necessity requires, from evil which threatens it from without by those of another nation. Or could we at all successfully maintain that war is good and justifiable if waged against evil subjects of one's own country, but that war becomes a moral evil the moment it is directed against iniquitous inhabitants of another country?

Justifiable Wars

It is, therefore, asserting too much to say that war in itself is evil. Such would be the case if all war were to be reduced to the one cause of malicious hatred and evil in the human heart. But there is not one cause of war in this world but two. The very first cause for war is the coexistence of the two opposing principles in the world; namely, the principles of righteousness and of iniquity, of truth and error, God and the devil. These can never live together in harmony. Evil by its very nature is hostile to truth and goodness and cares not for justice. When, therefore, evil will have its way and can not be cowed into submission by any other means, the use of armed force becomes inevitable. It then becomes the duty of all who love truth and righteousness and will stand for God's cause and human justice, to join in the armed resistance to evil. Hence, there are just wars in which we can and must at times engage.

On the other hand, wars can also originate in strife or greed or false ideals which run counter to truth and righteousness, and may be prompted by such evil motives in one or both contestants. It is not, therefore, necessarily true that one of the contestants is right. Both may be wrong and engage in warfare from wicked motives. On the other hand, when both are right there will be no war. In a world where the best of men is sinful there will always be sin attached to any war, as there is to all our deeds. Contrariwise, even in the basest of men there is always something left of God's common grace and his sin-restraining influence. Hence, it becomes the duty of men and of nations who would maintain justice to appeal to the instincts of common grace in those who would foment war, in the hope of averting bloodshed wherever possible, provided justice can, in the main, be preserved.

We have here, then, the principle which determines when a war is justifiable. It is right for a government to wage war when the principal end for which government is established by God, namely, the preservation of justice, cannot otherwise be maintained. Not all wars are justifiable. Many wars have been fought in history and are being fought today, in which the real motive is not the defense of justice, even though nations commonly make it the ostensible purpose, but some unrighteous gain. Even in cases where the cause itself is a just one, war is at times unjustifiable, because other avenues for the defense of justice have not been sufficiently exhausted before war was declared, such as arbitration. War should always be a last resort. Just wars are engaged in when for the maintenance of justice a nation must suppress an unjust rebellion; when it must of necessity wage war against another nation; when it must support a nation or its persecuted inhabitants; or when it must join a league in punitive action against unjust aggression.

War is, therefore, justifiable when it becomes necessary for the proper defense of justice. Other manifestly inadequate criteria have been used to determine the justifiability of war. A criterion often advanced is that defensive wars are justifiable, while offensive wars are not. This distinction has in its favor that it stigmatizes as evil the aggressor who seeks to encroach upon another's territory or rights. But it, nevertheless, fails as an exact criterion. Not all defensive wars can be termed just wars. It all depends upon what a nation is defending. It may, for example, be defending its hold upon a strip of land which it has previously taken from another country by fraud. When that other country later comes to claim its own and assume the role of aggressor, it would seem that the defender was unjust and the aggressor in his rights. This certainly would be true as long as the territory in dispute had not become the recognized possession of the other nation. Again, when one nation is violating the rights of another nation, even though not engaging in actual warfare, and all other means of averting the evil have been exhausted, it may become the duty of the other nation to assume the role of aggressor, and attack the one doing the injustice. Such instances are sufficient to indicate that the terms "defensive," "offensive," or "aggressive" warfare are inadequate distinctions.

Another criterion which has been suggested is that only "wars of Jehovah," those expressly bidden by God in the Bible, are just. This would stamp all wars of today as unjustifiable. But this criterion fails because it does not take into account the very reason why governments are instituted by God, as explained above. Even though no war today is expressly commanded by Jehovah, we must not forget that the government stands as God's agent to maintain justice with the sword. It has as its task both to determine when a war is justifiable and to wage warfare when the cause of justice would demand it in consonance with its divine behest.

Another faulty criterion would be that wars may be waged only for the sake of religion. If the government is established for the maintenance of justice, this would not only involve the cause of religious liberty, but also the independence of the fatherland, freedom from persecution, and in the main all sufficiently high moral values which cannot be preserved in any other way.

Proper Conduct of Belligerents

Thus we find that legitimate wars must be carried on by a lawful government and must be fought for the necessary maintenance of justice. There is besides these two factors a third consideration for legitimate warfare: the proper conduct of belligerents. We need to be reminded that there is a law of God which is in force in time of war as well as in time of peace, and that there are human rights which are to be respected. Belligerents must remain human, and not—as too often happens—lower themselves to the level of beasts. During war there is much temptation and much opportunity, both on the part of the military authorities and the soldiery, to do evil, either through the inhuman treatment of conquered enemies or of noncombatants, or by unnecessary bloodshed and destruction of property, and through all sorts of brutalities. It seems scarcely necessary to assert that all such outrages are contrary to the law of God and should be vigorously opposed. It is a sad travesty of Christian morals that Christian nations have frequently preserved little of the Christian spirit in time of war.

In addition to the proper conduct of those engaging in war, there are important ethical questions concerning the propriety of certain modes of warfare, types of bombs to be used and not to be used, bombardment of cities and villages not in the immediate war zone involving the lives of noncombatants, and other questionable tactics in wartime. But these questions involve too much technical knowledge to be discussed with profit here. It is at least a ray of hope that human instincts have led nations to come to somewhat of an understanding regarding certain practices which have thus far been outlawed in war. Further, it is a matter of singular importance to us that in the army the service of God be maintained through religious leaders such as army chaplains and through religious organizations, and that Christ as the Christian's Lord and King be recognized and obeyed while military service is rendered to the country.

A final matter in the Calvinist's attitude to war deals with the terms of peace in time of victory. If warfare may be engaged in only in defense of justice, it is a manifest misuse of victory for a conquering nation to avenge itself upon its enemy, or to endeavor to crush him or lord it over him. The ill-fated consequences of such abuse of a victor's power can be learned from the sad aftereffects of the Treaty of Versailles which closed the First World War. The purpose should be to establish an equitable peace and to secure the maintenance of justice. When this end has been established, the victorious nation should rest satisfied, and can rightfully ask no more.

From the foregoing discussion it is readily to be inferred how important, in fact how vital, it is that the nations of the world be permeated with the Christian spirit and have a sincere regard for the law of God. This is necessary not only for the determination of the just causes for war, but also for the proper prosecution of war and the conclusion of a righteous peace. The duty of the Christian to be the salt of the earth and the light of the world is, therefore, by no means small. Jesus is still the Savior, not only of the individual but also of society. Unless men and nations are willing to subject their wills to his teachings, to his Spirit, to himself, almost anything dreadful can happen to human society.

A question of great practical interest is the one which concerns a Christian's duty as citizen in the case of war. This involves the problem of the conscientious objector and it will be given special consideration in chapter 23.

22

The Christian and Total War

The appearance of techniques of mass destruction such as nuclear arms and chemical and biological weapons raises many new questions about warfare and the proper duty of governments. These weapons can lay waste to huge areas, perhaps even the earth itself, and invariably kill many noncombatants. Consequently, there must be grave doubts as to whether any war in which they are used could be legitimate. One nuclear bomb killed over one hundred thousand people at Hiroshima. The use of chlorine in the First World War and the use of chemical gases by Iraq against Iran and upon its own Kurdish population killed thousands of people in a matter of hours. The unfortunate victims had no chance to flee, or even to surrender. In the case of Hiroshima and the Kurds most of the dead were civilians who were owed protection under the international laws of war.

Certainly it is true that there has always been great bloodshed in war and that there have been wars of extermination in previous ages. Human sin always creates great evil. The Romans laid Jerusalem waste after its siege. The Mongols killed the inhabitants of cities that refused to surrender. Infectious diseases have been spread as a means of war. Even in the modern world the Nazis and the Khmer Rouge in Cambodia killed millions by much slower and more laborious means. The massacre of the innocent and the helpless is no new thing. In this sense the moral evil of the situation has not essentially changed in the modern age.

But one thing that has changed is modern science and technology. Our weapons are much more powerful and destructive, while at the same time much cheaper to acquire and easier to use than the weapons of former generations. At one time such destruction had to be carried out by many soldiers over months and years; but now it can be accomplished by a few people in a matter of hours. At one time it could be done only by the very powerful; but now even a small nation can acquire such means. The very power of such weapons hinders and even prevents a purely local attack on an enemy army; they necessarily kill and destroy more widely. This tremendous power also means that the progress of any nuclear war is unpredictable and probably uncontrollable. Most knowledgeable observers believe that there is little or no possibility of containing a nuclear war once it has begun. It will likely be played out to the destruction of all human and nonhuman life. It was this realization that led Secretary Gorbachev of the Soviet Union and President Reagan of the United States to declare jointly in their 1988 summit that "a nuclear war can never be won and must never be fought." Clearly these new weapons of mass destruction pose a new set of problems to which we as Christians must respond in addressing the question of war.

Judging the New Weapons

While there is much that is new in warfare we may still approach these problems in terms of the biblical view of war outlined in previous chapters. It was pointed out that Christians can and should engage only in wars that are just. For such a war to be legitimate it must be waged by a lawful government; it must be carried out only for the preservation of justice; it may be launched only if justice cannot otherwise be preserved; and it must be engaged in only as a last resort—if and when all other means, such as negotiation or arbitration or international law or peaceful sanctions, have failed.

But apart from the justifiability before God of the war itself, the actual *conduct* of the war must be proper. It is the *means* of fighting that the Calvinist must question. The law of God is never abrogated and must be followed even in conflict, difficult through this might seem. Enemies must be respected as human beings and not treated inhumanely. The means used to wage war must be in proportion to the goals of the war. The war itself must not to a greater harm in order to achieve a smaller good. We may not kill thousands in order to save the lives of ten. Prisoners must be treated humanely and noncombatants must be protected and shielded from attack. Existing laws and treaties, such as the Hague and Geneva Conventions on the rules of war, must be obeyed. The victory aimed at must not be the extermination of our enemies but their return to a proper place within the world. The earth itself must be safeguarded in war. In the Old Testament God called upon Israel not to destroy the trees but only to use those which they needed, asking "are the trees in the field men, that they should be besieged by thee?" (Deut. 20:19, 20).

In earlier ages it was possible to exterminate one's enemies even while using only very primitive weapons such as rifles or swords. But at least such weapons did not *have* to be used in such an atrocious way. It was possible also to use a rifle or sword in a more legitimate fashion. The problem with nuclear, chemical, and biological weapons is that they can only be used in an indiscriminate way, for they are inherently massive in their effects. Nerve gases blanket the landscape and kill or maim anybody who comes into contact with them—like the Kurdish villagers of Iraq in recent years. Nuclear weapons explode with the force of thousands of tons of TNT, and so their use necessarily levels a large area, killing—quickly or slowly—almost everyone and everything within that area. They cannot be used in a way that protects noncombatants. They necessarily destroy the land of an enemy. Therefore, no war involving the use of nuclear weapons could meet the principles we have outlined for the proper conduct of belligerents in a legitimate war. No war which would annihilate humankind, or leave alive only a wretched fragment of it, could respect the lives of the innocent, honor existing laws of war, achieve a just peace with the enemy, or return an aggressor to its rightful place among the nations. Such weapons cannot be used in a just and legitimate way. If we submit ourselves to the Word of God, then we must resist the idea of fighting with nuclear, chemical, biological, or other weapons of mass destruction.

War in the Modern World

What we have said about the use of nuclear weapons does not mean that war itself is always wrong in this age. Rather it means that waging war with nuclear or other means of mass destruction is wrong. In fact there have been many wars during what we call the "nuclear age" which have not involved such weapons or the threat of their use. If the goal of the war is legitimate, the means are properly limited, and no other means are possible, then it may still be justifiable for a modern state to engage in war.

However, the presence of nuclear weapons still casts a long shadow even over those conflicts which do not involve their use and which may otherwise be just. This is especially true if one or more of the combatants possesses nuclear weapons, even though they do not use them and are committed to not using them. This is because the tension, fear, and pride present in any war increase the danger that someone will be tempted to use these weapons. In a world corrupted by sin we cannot ignore this possibility even though it would almost certainly be an act not only of destruction but of *self*-destruction. Such a temptation may be very strong for a country that is losing in a conventional conflict; it may face intense pressure to switch to nuclear combat.

For these reasons, while there may still be justifiable war in the nuclear age, all war now takes place in a more dangerous situation. The possibility of being drawn into a nuclear conflict makes it even more urgent that any war be avoided whenever and wherever possible.

The Christian's Duty

Given the dangers of modern means of mass destruction, it is our Christian duty to condemn the use of such weapons in war and to reaffirm God's requirements for the just conduct of war. We must also actively strive to prevent the outbreak of any war which could involve the use of nuclear weapons, and we must seek to end our dependence on them. We should not do these things because of any belief that the world is really a peace-loving place, that humankind can fundamentally transform itself, that nations will forsake self-interest, or that a utopia free from all war can be achieved. None of these things is true, and such perfection awaits the final reign of the Messiah. Our concern is not prompted by optimism or pacifism. Rather, the Calvinist's desire to limit the nuclear threat stems precisely from the recognition that all people are sinful and that, therefore, there is a real danger that nuclear arms will be used. We are motivated by our commitment to uphold the limits that God puts on war.

While an appeal for self-control can and should be made to the consciences of leaders, especially in countries that have been shaped by the Christian faith, we must also call for the formation of appropriate international law. We need to develop laws and treaties that limit the nuclear threat. Such treaties should limit the number, type, and location of weapons. In order to be effective they must also provide a means of detecting any violations, so there need to be inspection systems and safeguards. Another requirement is incentives or sanctions to guarantee adherence to the terms of the treaty. These should involve, at the mildest level, public opinion or peaceful sanctions such as trade embargoes. But by and large the major sanction and threat stem from the weapons themselves. Any country which uses nuclear weapons is liable to be destroyed itself and so each country shares an interest in limiting and removing such weapons. In a sense each country has become its own hostage.

It would be better if these treaties and safeguards could be properly administered by an international body such as the United Nations or the World Court. But at present such bodies do not have the resources for either administration or enforcement of such treaties. In addition the number of countries that possess nuclear weapons is relatively small, and the number seeking to limit and reduce them is even smaller. For this reason the most effective negotiations have involved only the nuclear powers. The usual format has been negotiations between the United States and the Soviet Union, or else between NATO and the Warsaw Pact countries. In the present situation Christians should strongly encourage and pray for such bilateral efforts. For this reason we commend efforts to establish treaties to limit antiballistic missiles and intermediate-range missiles. At this time we are particularly grateful to God for the major efforts underway to further reduce nuclear weaponry.

The Continuing Danger

It may be that by God's grace nuclear and other devastating weapons will be reduced to zero. But even then their threat will not have totally passed. It seems unlikely that we will forget how to build such weapons and so the possibility of their resurgence will always remain. Not only their possession but even their actual invention has fundamentally altered international relations. This is why treaties need to be safeguarded by rigorous inspection—to prevent people not only from concealing weapons but also from taking steps to rebuild them. Even then the threat will not totally disappear. Consequently, it is ever more urgent to leaven our international affairs with the gospel of the Prince of Peace. We will need continually to pray to God to preserve us from destruction, and we will need always to remember that our hope lies not in humankind's greatness but in God's promises and grace.

23

The Christian Citizen and War

The Christian's duty with regard to war is of momentous interest at any time, for war always involves the question of hardship and privation and even the possible loss of life. But it is especially important today now that military service is required of vast numbers of our young men, and world tensions remain.

The Christian's Duty Prior to War

A very first duty of the Christian in regard to war—in fact a most vital one—concerns his conduct in time of peace, before a war has begun. It is decidedly a Christian's duty to help prevent war. An ounce of prevention is always worth a pound of cure. Christians have in their possession the mightiest weapon to counteract war that is known to mankind. Rightly understood, the Christian church member belongs to the best pacifist society on earth. He need not join a pacifist organization for distribution of antiwar propaganda in order to promote peace among the nations. Pacifist movements have their value in focusing attention upon the horrors of war, but they are not able to effect a cure for the war germ which lies concealed in the hearts of men.

We can perhaps learn a lesson from the many pacifist societies which existed prior to the First World War. Ever since 1848, when the czar of Russia published his pacifist manifesto bearing the slogan "In the name of humanity, no more murders," countless pacifist organizations have held conventions. In 1898 the First International Peace Conference was held at The Hague. In 1907 a second conference was held. And in 1914, at the completion of the Peace Palace at The Hague, another International Peace Conference was staged. Official representatives from twenty different nations assembled to help celebrate what was supposed to be the inauguration of a new era in the life of humanity. War had come to an end. But scarcely had this peace conference concluded its sessions when a war of stupendous dimensions broke out. And these same pacifists participated not only in the war, but also in the mutual hatreds. Many professors disowned the honorary degrees which they had received from universities in opposing nations. Two noted scientists, who were also noted pacifists, wrote an open letter in the Berliner *Tageblatt* of August 19, 1914, scathingly denouncing England's "inextinguishable shame" in causing the war. The effect of the pacifist propaganda seemed to vanish into thin air overnight. Some still retained the hope that this would be a war to end war, but this also in time turned out to be nothing more than a delusion.

Christians still have in their church the most effective pacifist organization in existence. The most effective weapon with which to counteract war lies precisely in the Christian gospel. Jesus Christ is today, as he was proclaimed of old, the great Prince of Peace and the Savior of human society. The Calvinistic political party of Holland, known as the Anti-Revolutionary party, has inscribed in its banner the slogan: "Over against revolution the gospel." We would do well in counteracting the evil of war to adopt that motto in modified form as our pacifist cry: "Over against war the gospel." We should combat the war spirit, not with the merely humanistic propaganda of the pacifist, but by disseminating the Christian gospel. The Christian in counteracting war should himself be a militant soldier, using as his sword the sword of the Spirit, which is the Word of God. What is of even greater value, he should himself become in all his living more distinctively Christian, drawing upon the Spirit of Christ to allay the war spirit in his own breast. Endowed with a goodly measure of the Spirit of the Prince of Peace, who is at the same time the Prince of Truth and Righteousness, the Christian becomes a most mighty agent for the promotion of peace and righteousness in this world. When so endowed and having imbibed the Spirit of Christ, he becomes a true pacifist and can in this respect answer to the calling to be the salt of the earth and the light of a war-darkened world. On the other hand, when Christianity itself drifts away from Christ and becomes colorless, it loses its power for peace and righteousness; then the type of political leader and henchman who would ignore the demands of justice for political advantage becomes bold, and the dove of peace can find no rest for the hollow of its foot. The apparently total disregard for what is right on the part of many today stands directly related to the departure of the true Christian spirit from the community.

The Christian's Duty during War

Besides the duty to avert war by the inculcation of Christian principles and the dissemination of the Christian spirit through the gospel, the Christian citizen also has a duty once war is declared. The government will issue a call to arms to defend the country. What must be the citizen's attitude toward his country's call? For a proper determination of his duty it is necessary to keep several facts in mind. It is first of all necessary to remember the general principle that a citizen is in duty bound to obey his government, being subject to the higher powers for God's sake. Speaking generally, it is not within the province of the private citizen to decide whether he will obey his government or not. The duty of a Christian citizen in the case of a call to arms does not differ essentially from the obligation which he has to obey the government in any given case.

A second factor to be remembered is that the government's authority over the citizen is not absolute but subject to definite limitations. The government may not interfere with anything which rightfully belongs to the internal order of the home or of the church or of any other sphere in human society, but is limited to its own sphere and to the administration of civic affairs. Furthermore, in the realm of the spirit it finds its limits in conscience. Genuine matters of conscience must have the respect and, insofar as possible, the protection of the government. Nevertheless, within its own rightful domain the government must be scrupulously obeyed, out of the highest motive, for God's sake.

Another significant fact is that it is the government's duty to decide upon war, not that of the private citizen. To declare war is distinctly a matter which belongs to the government's jurisdiction, for which it is given the power of the sword. It is not the duty of the private citizen to help the government decide by popular vote when a war is to be declared, or when it is to be considered a just war. Only insofar as it concerns the private citizen himself as a possible participant, because it involves the matter of conscience to obey God above all in all walks of life, will the private citizen have the duty for himself to answer the question whether it is a justifiable war to which he is called and in which he can conscientiously take part.

Even though the private citizen may desire to determine the justifiability of war, he will soon discover that in many, if not in most cases, he will lack the necessary data upon which to base a just and adequate opinion. Usually in the tense days just preceding a war, partisan propaganda plays an important role, thereby beclouding the issue between the nations which are at odds. Moreover, many important facts upon which a proper opinion must necessarily be based are not available to the public. Even the historian, who in later years seeks to determine the causes of the war after he has collected all available data, often finds it most difficult to render a just and impartial decision. At the present time it is still a matter much in dispute where to fix the blame for the First World War. If then the professional historian, with all the evidence at his command can with difficulty determine the justifiability of a modern war, it becomes extremely difficult for a private citizen to render a just decision at the time a war is to be declared. Nevertheless, the citizen needs just that evidence, for the burden of proof lies with him if he is to deviate from the position of his government and decide that the war is unjustifiable. Only when the Christian judges the war to be unjustifiable, so that he would sin against God if he participated, can he in conscience refuse to obey his government as the authority placed over him, in favor of obedience to the higher Authority, God.

The Conscientious Objector

Despite the fact, however, that it is difficult for a citizen to have the necessary information at hand on which a conscientious objection should be based, there will always be conscientious objectors with whom the government must reckon. The government is placed in authority by God. When a citizen questions its right to make a demand by an appeal to a contradictory demand of the higher authority of God, it becomes a matter of serious concern to the government to inquire whether it has not exceeded its authority and exacted something which God has expressly forbidden. Not only must the government respect the consciences of its citizens; but in the United States and in certain other countries, it does respect them. Not only has the government made provision for exemption from military service for religious sects as the Quakers, who claim all war to be unlawful; but it exempts from the demand of oathtaking in civil courts those who for conscience's sake may not swear oaths, and excuses from vaccination schoolchildren whose parents have religious scruples against the practice.

The determinative question here is: What constitutes a conscientious objector? Can any man who has a serious difference of opinion with his government about war qualify as a conscientious objector? This important question can only be decided by a proper understanding of conscience. By conscience we understand the moral consciousness of man, whereby he judges his own opinions and deeds according to the inborn moral law. This does not make conscience itself the last court of appeal or the norm or standard which decides questions of human conduct. It is always the moral law itself which is the last court of appeal, to which the conscience of man knows itself in duty bound. This moral law presupposes a Lawgiver and Judge, who is the Author and Defender of that moral law. This Author is none less than God himself. According to Calvinistic opinion this moral law finds its clear and objective interpretation in the revealed will of God found in Scripture. The Bible then becomes for fallen man the norm or standard by which the consciences of both civil officials and citizens are to be regulated.

It may be objected that many officials and citizens do not recognize the existence of God or the authority of the Word of God and will not be governed by such considerations. However, as Holland's former prime minister, Hendrik Colyn, has stated,[1] while the government officials or citizens may ignore or even be hostile to God's Word, the ordinances of God and the duty to conform to them remain. We as Christians may never yield to the notion that men are free to disregard God's Word the moment they do not believe it, any more than did the apostles or the Christian martyrs of past ages. These always insisted on conformity even of pagans to God's written will. Instead of relinquishing the demand that God be recognized as the supreme Ruler and his Word as the ultimate norm of human conduct, Christians should seek to exert a moral influence to develop this consciousness in the public mind. It is a matter of common observation that conscience diminishes in effectiveness in the measure that the bond which binds men to God and to his Word is no longer felt by the people.

Conscience, then, if rightly interpreted, knows itself in duty bound to the moral law of God as the supreme adjudicator of life. For this very reason there must be freedom of conscience. This fact lies in the peculiar nature of conscience itself. For conscience is that element in man's soul which places him in the sacred presence of God himself. When this occurs, all human word, all human authority, even of those who are placed by God in an office above us, must for the individual concerned step aside. It is not to be wondered at that freedom of conscience is a basic principle of Protestantism and has won its way to recognition through a history of blood.

From the study of conscience it becomes clear that not all objections to war, however sincere these may be, can be registered as conscientious objections. Materialistic socialists and communists do not even believe in God. Others, though they do acknowledge the existence and even the authority of God, may object to war on merely political or economic or humanitarian grounds. The right of such citizens to endeavor to bring the government to their point of view by orderly constitutional procedure ought always to be recognized. But it would be beclouding the issue to term such differences of opinion conscientious objections. The government may never exempt a citizen from the obligation to observe its laws because of a mere subjective difference of opinion about their wisdom. Conscience always implies the existence of an authority higher than the government, because of which the government's authority must step aside. And no higher authority exists in such cases.

The grounds on which conscientious objectors claim exemption from military duty are not the same in all cases. These may be grouped under the following three heads. A first group claims exemption on the ground that they are members of religious organizations whose faith forbids the taking up of arms in any war. To this group belong the Friends (commonly known as Quakers) and the Mennonites. A second group includes those members of a religious denomination which, while not condemning war as a group, has nevertheless officially endorsed the rights of conscientious objectors in their membership, as for example, the Episcopalians, and to a certain extent the Methodists. The churches of Calvinistic persuasion, as the Reformed and the Presbyterian, cannot be classified with either of these groups. We of Calvinistic belief hold with the Westminister Confession[2] that the government may engage in war "upon just and necessary occasion." A third group includes those conscientious objectors who claim the right to decide as individuals whether they find the war just or not, irrespective of the view of their denomination. A familiar example of this last group is the case of the Canadian professor D. C. Macintosh of Yale Divinity School. He was a member of a Baptist church, a denomination which admits the justifiability of war. While he himself was not a pacifist, having served as chaplain in the First World War, he, in applying for United States citizenship, wanted to reserve the right for himself to determine whether a given war was unjust, in which case he asked exemption from military duty on this ground. His application was denied by the United States Supreme Court by a vote of five to four.[3]

The vexing problem here concerns the difficulty of determining how respect for the conscientious objections of a citizen is to be combined with the duty of the government in the case of war. For the conscientious objections of citizens do not affect merely the individuals themselves, but also the domain of the government. The government also has its conscience, by virtue of which it will consider itself conscience bound to make certain demands and maintain certain standards. It is a fact that both in nonmilitary and military affairs scruples of conscientious objectors may jeopardize the political order or public morals. A striking example is found in the conscientious objections of certain Anabaptists of former days to the wearing of any clothing. Quite naturally the government had the duty to prohibit these conscientious objectors from appearing in the nude when in public.

Likewise in the case of war, the government may consider that it has the duty to call its citizens to arms. But the conscientious objectors may view it their duty to refuse to serve. In the case of any such apparent clash of moral duties, what must a government do? It may not ignore the sincere conscientious scruples of its religious citizens. On the other hand, it may not jeopardize the welfare of the country or shirk its imperative duty of prosecuting the war. The solution to this knotty problem which has been given in the past by our country is perhaps the only just and equitable one; namely, that the government, while not excusing such conscientious objectors from service to the country, nevertheless assign to them duties which do not carry them out to the battlefront.

In the event, however, that a government should not hesitate, for whatsoever reason, to override the conscience of its citizen, and the citizen finds it in conscience impossible to do military duty because it would violate the solemn duty which he owes to his God, what then must the citizen do? There is apparently but one answer to this vital question. It is the answer which Peter and John gave to the religious and civil authorities of the Sanhedrin at Jerusalem: "Whether it be right in the sight of God to harken unto you more than unto God, judge ye" (Acts 4:19). But then with those same apostles and the many Christian martyrs, the conscientious objector should be ready to face the consequence either of fines, or imprisonment, or even death. For, regardless of the cost, no one may in conscience violate what he perceives to be the will of God.

24

Liberation Theology

Throughout history Christians have been concerned with the relation between the gospel of Jesus Christ and injustice in human society. Augustine, the greatest theologian in the early centuries of Christendom, wrestled with this question in his monumental work *The City of God.* In medieval times, Thomas Aquinas devoted much of his work to it, and religious orders, such as the Franciscans, developed out of a commitment to minister to the poor. Nor have Calvinists been reticent in these matters. Calvin himself worked to alleviate the plight of refugees and other poor people in Geneva. Around the turn of this century, the great Dutch Calvinist leader Abraham Kuyper brought "the social question" to the forefront of the issues facing the Calvinistic political parties. He declared "that the direct relation between the social question and the Christian religion is simply *undeniable.*"[1]

With suffering and injustice so widespread throughout the world Christians today are focusing much more attention on these problems. One of the major centers of thought and action dealing with these issues has been Latin America, particularly the Roman Catholic Church there, and one of the major results of this emphasis is what is now often called "political theology" or, more commonly, "liberation theology." The proponents of this type of theology emphasize that it has grown out of profound experiences of suffering and oppression. They assert that the fundamental characteristics of many Latin American societies are widespread poverty and malnutrition, vast disparities in wealth, and governments, including military dictatorships, which are unwilling or unable to do much about the situation. Many priests maintain that their training and theological education are foreign to this reality and relate to a world different from the one in which they are actually living.

Many priests working to relieve suffering discover that their duties often lead to political involvement. They might, for example, work pastorally with a family where the husband has disappeared or been killed. But when several, or many, husbands disappear then a pastor's training is totally inadequate. Liberation theologians maintain that what is required is a political movement. They claim that, since politics and economics dominate the situation, then a Christian understanding (a "theology") oriented to politics and economics and directed to overcoming oppression is necessary. This type of theology is called "liberation theology."

Parallel movements have developed among Christians in other parts of the world as well. They are present in Asia and in Africa. In South Africa liberation theology has developed among Christian opponents of the apartheid policy of the National party, and there the theology has taken on a particular Calvinist hue. A similar development has also come about in the Western world, though in these areas, apart from the development of "black theology," it is more a movement of students, theologians, and church officials rather than the population at large.

Liberation theologians especially in Latin America stress the centrality of justice in the gospel and have taken the image of the unjustly treated, crucified Savior as their central symbol. They emphasize that theology cannot be an abstract, objective pursuit but must be oriented to the actual lives of the poor, must come out of an experience of oppression, and must be oriented toward liberation. They hold that abstract talk of liberation is not sufficient and that theology itself must be supplemented by social, political, and economic analyses. Because it is believed that Marxism is often shaped by an overriding concern for justice, the analysis taken is commonly a Marxist one. Hence many, though certainly not all, liberation theologians try to make use of Marxism in terms of "tools of social analysis"—as a means of understanding power relations in society—while emphasizing that they do not accept Marxism as a worldview.

There are common themes in liberation theology throughout the world, and we shall look at these shortly. But we should not emphasize only what unifies the movement for, together with what is common to all, there are also very great differences. Apart from different countries and areas and continents, there are also variations even within countries. Some theologians accept the possibility of violence while others are determinedly nonviolent. Some are revolutionary, some are not. Some have a leaning toward Marxism, some do not. Some are Protestants, and this moves them away from the theological pattern of traditional Roman Catholics. Others are Calvinists. Hence, in describing liberation theology, we must be aware that we are not describing a unified organization with rules, or a church with creeds, but a very diverse movement. None of the praise or criticism we make of it will apply equally to all branches of the movement. We can only hope to describe and evaluate the overall general pattern.

Strengths of Liberation Theology

Liberation theology has many strengths that Calvinists can endorse. These can best be seen in what Calvinism and liberation theology jointly reject rather than in what they affirm. Liberation theology rejects the idea that the salvation we have in Jesus Christ is solely a matter of another world, as though we are elect in Christ merely to escape from this world. It emphasizes instead that salvation extends to every part of our present being; we are not called to escape from the world but to live unto God throughout and within this world. We belong to and are renewed in Christ—body, soul, and spirit. Liberation theologians reject the view that this world is of no importance to God and instead affirm that the entire world is God's and that God's hand is upon it. They reject the view that politics is necessarily unchristian or neutral and so should be avoided by Christians; they affirm instead that politics is a central and vital part of God's world and that political activity is a means of Christian service. They reject the view that poverty and injustice are the natural lot of humankind and the view that God is not concerned with poverty; instead, they affirm that God is concerned with the poor and calls for justice for the poor. As they point out, Amos denounces those "who oppress the poor, who crush the needy" (Amos 4:1), while Isaiah condemns those who "turn aside the needy from justice" (Isa. 10:1–4). The psalmist praises the Lord "who executes justice for the oppressed; who gives food to the hungry" (Ps. 146:7). Kuyper too emphasized this: "The worker must be able to live as one created in the image of God. . . . God's word itself gives him the right . . . to indict a social arrangement which makes him so painfully go without."[2]

Liberation theology is in many ways a departure from traditional Roman Catholic views. Traditionally, Roman Catholicism divides the world into a realm of nature and a realm of grace. The realm of nature is the realm of "the world"—the realm of the human body, of reason, of science, of politics. The realm of grace is the realm of the Spirit, of prayer, of holiness, of the church. The gospel is thought to apply only to the second of these realms, the realm of grace. This realm is treated as the exclusive focus of biblical teaching and the arena of distinctive Christian service. The realm of nature, on the other hand, is an area shared with those who are not Christian. The principles of this area are supposed to be found in natural human reason and are accessible to and shared equally by Christians and non-Christians. It is supposedly a neutral realm about which Christians have nothing specifically Christian to say.

Protestantism was in many ways a criticism of and an attempt to overcome this Catholic division of the world. The Reformation emphasized God's concern for all of life. Liberation theology has developed a similar criticism of the traditional Catholic narrowing of the scope of the gospel and has reemphasized the importance for Christians of renewing the political world. In this and other ways it shows parallels to Protestantism.

Another major virtue of liberation theology is that it highlights the non-Western world. Most Christians in the world now live in Asia, Africa, and Latin America. The churches in these areas are often vigorous and growing and are rapidly on their way to becoming the central force in the Christian world, if, indeed, they are not already so. Yet too often our Western view of the church, theology, and the problems facing Christians still takes Europe or North America as its center or model. Liberation theology reminds us that the Word of the

Lord is universal and that the church, too, is universal. There are more black Calvinists than white ones in South Africa. There are more Reformed Christians in Korea than in North America. The Western world must therefore not only try to teach, but also learn from the rest of the world.

Yet another strength of liberation theology is that it challenges us to take our commitment to justice seriously. This emphasis is not new to historic Calvinism. As Kuyper put it, "it must be admitted to our shame, that the Roman Catholics are far ahead of us in their study of the social question." He believed that "the sixth commandment, thou shalt not kill—includes killing the worker socially."[3] Liberation theology teaches much that Christians should respect. It should also cause us to pay more serious attention to cries for justice from within the Calvinist tradition itself.

Weaknesses of Liberation Theology

Despite its strengths and its needed correction of past Christian errors, liberation theology is not something that the Calvinist can wholeheartedly embrace. While such theology correctly exposes many problems, some of its solutions to those problems frequently seem to draw little from the Scriptures.

While liberation theologians correctly claim that the gospel deals with justice in this world, they sometimes seem to imply that the gospel deals *only* with this issue—that our restoration in Jesus Christ is the same as a new political and social order, and that the kingdom of God is a renewed society. Against a one-sided flight from this world some reduce God's promises to this world. They lose God's transcendence and the need for humankind to be reconciled with God as well as with one another. Against this, the Reformed Christian must emphasize that while a life lived out of Jesus Christ can and must lead to renewal in society, it is much more than a program of political change. At its heart is the restoration of our relationship with God, out of which all new life can come.

A second problem is that, after conceptualizing the gospel in terms of the social needs of this world, some liberation theologians treat these needs almost exclusively in terms of politics. The key to all real change is held to be political change. The these needs almost exclusively in terms of politics. The key to all real change is held to be political change. The key to overcoming injustice and oppression is to be found in political power. Calvinists have no problem stressing the importance of politics and the vital position of political leaders. Calvin himself described the role of the magistrate as "not only holy and legitimate, but also the most sacred and honourable in human life."[4] Certainly God places great power in the hand of the state, and he calls on the state to correct injustice. But as we have seen, no state can or should try to correct everything that is wrong. It must respect the office and calling of others in society. If the principle of sphere sovereignty is violated, then even more injustice and suffering will follow. If we are concerned to do justice and fight oppression, we must reject any attempt to deify the state or to look to "the people" as the source of all wisdom and righteousness.

A third problem with liberation theology is a tendency to use Marxist tools of social analysis as a means of understanding society, politics, and economics. It is certainly true that we need to understand society. We cannot deal with injustice solely in terms of biblical texts or systematic theology; there needs to be a real analysis of social relations themselves. It is certainly also true that there is much to be learned from Marx; Kuyper called him "a man of outstanding learning and high scholarly sense."[5] But Christians cannot just take over a Marxist (or liberal or conservative) view of the nature of society and assume that it is an adequate guide to action. Just as nothing in the world is neutral with respect to God, so no science can be neutral. Each social science reflects, in large part, the religious beliefs and commitments of those who have developed and used it. Our way of understanding society always depends on our view of human nature, sin, the direction of history, the purpose of the world, and our hopes for the future. A Marxist analysis is always dependent on the worldview of Marxism and will tend to commit those who use it to certain false assumptions (such as the perfectability of humankind, the driving force of history, or the necessity of socialism) whether they are aware of it or not. While there are things to learn from Marxism, it must be remembered that its goal is that "man will revolve about himself as his own true sun." We cannot take over parts of its system without, at the same time, being partly taken over by that system with its belief that "it is the solution to the riddle of history."[6] Instead we need analyses of society that spring from and reflect a Christian view of the world.

One of the effects produced by these emphases within liberation theology is its claim that God is, and therefore we should be, on the side of the poor. We must be very careful of any criticism here, for we must never turn away from the poor. The Lord cares for the poor and emphasizes repeatedly that he watches over the poor and that his hand is always upon them. God is a God who defends and redeems the poor. As Kuyper says, "When rich and poor stand opposed to each other God never takes his place with the wealthier, but always stands with the poorer."[7] One of the major virtues of liberation theology is that it has shown the centrality of the theme of the poor in the Bible. But despite these emphases, we do not find the phrase, or the intent, in the Bible that God is *"on the side of* the poor." Such an expression implies that there is a certain kind of conflict going on and that God is taking the side of a particular class of human beings. In Scripture, however, God has a law or standard of justice by which all conflicts are judged and oppression is corrected. In terms of this standard, we seek to rectify injustice. While such rectifying will always mean defending and succoring the poor, this does not mean that God is *on a particular side.* In this instance it appears that liberation theology's dependence on Marxism has caused it to distort one theme of the biblical message.

Hence, while we can see that there is much to applaud in liberation theology, it is not a trend we can easily follow. Some liberation theologians seem to adopt a pattern in which following Jesus Christ almost becomes reduced to fighting for a particular political ideology. But no ideology, whether left- or right-wing, can be seen as the essence of the gospel.

Coming to Terms with Liberation Theology

We have said that there are things to be learned and things to be rejected in liberation theology. But we must be careful that we do not reject something simply because it threatens our privileged position. In the words of Kuyper, "There is no place here for those who would march in the ranks with us because they fear that their money box is in danger."[8] We must listen to criticism of ourselves and hear the voice of those who are oppressed.

What we must reject in liberation theology is any tendency to reduce the gospel to a horizontal dimension based on the claim that our relation with God is reducible to our relation with others, any tendency to adopt a view of the world shaped by Marxism, and any tendency to see the state as the basic and final solution to human problems. Each of these is a departure from a biblical worldview.

But what we must accept is its concern for this world, the call to do justice, the realization that God is vitally concerned with the needs of the poor, and its understanding that one of the most important tasks of government is to combat injustice in society. These are tenets of historic Calvinism which we must boldly affirm and reaffirm.

It is not enough, however, that we declare this truth; we must also seek to live by its light. Faith without works is dead, and claims of justice without deeds of justice are a violation of Holy Scripture and of the Reformed faith. As Kuyper declared in 1891 to the First Christian Social Congress, "Have you the right to take your ease as long as this society remains—even though there be state intervention—not again re-patterned according to God's Word?"[9]

25

Political Hope

As we approach the twenty-first century, both good and evil flourish. Many people are starving, while at the same time there are great increases in the availability of food. There are weapons that can destroy the world coupled with treaties that can help bring a proper unity to the world. Our century has witnessed the extermination of millions of people in Nazi Germany, in Stalinist Russia, in nationalist Turkey, and in Communist Cambodia, but it also declares the universal rights of every human being. In the Western world the impact of Christianity has been steadily decreasing; our society seems ever more alienated from the Word of God. Yet we also live in one of the greatest ages of missionary expansion in the history of the church. In so far as we can judge, the number of Christians in the world is increasing and the gospel is spreading quickly over the continents. We do not know whether by God's grace this growth will continue, or whether the secularization that infects the West will also weaken Christian witness in other parts of the world.

The corrupting effects of sin are manifest in the cruelty and perversion of a humanity that tries to live apart from and against the Lord. But because our world is still sustained by the grace of God, these effects of sin are restrained. Our world is not abandoned to the devil; everywhere there are signs of hope and healing as the creation is continually preserved by God's mercy. Simply in terms of our own experience we can say neither that the situation in the world is getting worse nor that things are steadily improving as though humankind were moving toward the kingdom of God. Instead there is the coexistence and conflict of good and evil, of the kingdom of God and the kingdom of this world. In this age we see signs neither of final defeat nor of imminent victory. Rather we see an ongoing, and even sharpening, struggle.

The Scriptures lead us to expect such a struggle. The Calvinist is not overwhelmed by forebodings that the world will soon slide into destruction, nor puffed up by the expectation that the church will immediately triumph over the forces of darkness, although either of these is possible in the providence of God. We now live "between the times," between the first and second coming of our Lord Jesus Christ. In this time good and evil coexist and God continues to send rain upon the just and the unjust. The wheat and the tares grow up side by side and intermingle until the day of judgment (Matt. 13:30).

The Continuing Effects of Sin

Governing a huge country and managing the massive organization of a modern state would be tasks difficult enough even if there were no sin in the world. The impact of sin makes our political task seem almost impossible. The Calvinist's belief in total depravity means that we can never have naive or utopian expectations in politics. No activity in the world can of itself overcome sin but will itself be tainted by sin. We cannot give ourselves to a shallow optimism; we must be sober judges of the aptitudes, failures, and accomplishments of humankind.

Hence we must treat all programs for an ideal society skeptically. Certainly we are called to be fully Christian in all that we do, and we are promised that God's hand will be upon us for good in everything. But this is not meant to be a guarantee of immediate success, in politics or in anything else. Too often Christians have believed that they could institute a fully Christian political order on earth. The Roman emperor Constantine thought this when he sought to make the empire officially Christian. Many other Christian political approaches have also ended in failure. The Jesuits struggled and eventually failed to establish a Christian order in Paraguay. Numerous sects in North America in the nineteenth and twentieth centuries have striven to erect pure, alternative Christian societies.

Calvinists have not been immune to such plans. The Puritans of New England and Calvin in Geneva often found their efforts at political reform frustrated and corrupted.

Though God calls us to be genuinely Christian in politics, he does not give us guarantees of easy, clear, or simple solutions—or even of any solutions at all. Our life as Christians is simply one of taking up the vocation that God has given us, humbly and obediently. The ultimate consequences of what we do lie with the Lord. God does not promise us earthly success nor does he even call us to such success. We are not given goals to be achieved; we are simply called to follow in his ways. As Jesus says in the Sermon on the Mount, "Do not be anxious about your life, what you shall eat or what you shall drink, nor about your body, what you shall put on. . . . But seek first his kingdom and his righteousness, and all these things shall be yours as well. . . . Do not be anxious about tomorrow, for tomorrow will be anxious for itself. Let the day's own trouble be sufficient for the day" (Matt. 6:25–34). Jesus' words are a rebuke to every kind of pride or overconfidence. He calls us daily to seek to do justice and he promises that God's blessing will follow. We do not *make* good things happen; instead, we are called to be obedient servants, trusting that whatever happens is in God's hands and that he may be pleased to use our efforts.

Political Hopes

Although we must avoid every kind of utopianism and false expectation, this does not mean that we are called to act in politics without any hope at all. We have much hope. First of all, we have a secure ultimate hope since Jesus told his disciples, and through them tells us, "Be of good cheer, I have overcome the world" (John 16:33). We know that there will be new heavens and a new earth wherein righteousness dwells. Inscribed upon the headquarters of the United Nations building in New York are the words of Isaiah's vision of the coming reign of the Messiah: "They shall beat their swords into ploughshares, and their spears into pruning hooks; nation shall not lift up sword against nation, neither shall they learn war any more" (Isa. 2:4). The United Nations may not achieve this goal, but Jesus Christ will. While the fulfilment of this promise awaits his return, yet the steadfast knowledge that it will come about can fill everything that we do with hope and anchor all our actions in the certainty of God's abiding faithfulness. It will help us to be unbowed and unafraid as we face the difficult struggles of the present age.

Even beyond these future hopes, however, we have great comfort even in what God is doing here and now. The new world that will appear will bear the marks of this world. When the apostle Peter writes that "the heavens and earth that now exist have been stored up for fire" (2 Pet. 3:7), he not only portrays the destruction and end of this world; he also draws an explicit parallel to the tribulation and "destruction" of the world at the time of Noah. With Noah the Lord did not end the world but purified it and saved a remnant. Peter makes the same point by using the image of the refiner's fire which separates the pure from the impure. Peter is saying that the principalities and powers of this age and world rulers opposed to God will pass away, while genuine works of faithfulness and righteousness will endure. The Lord's refining fire will burn up the chaff but the good wheat will be carried into his barn (Matt. 13:24–30; 3:12; Luke 12:49). Those things that we do which spring genuinely from the grace and mercy of God and which are done in faith and obedience will not pass away and be lost forever. Instead they will be purified and will be carried over into the kingdom of God. Our present faithful actions will make a difference for eternity.[1]

But even beyond this hope for the future we have hope in this present generation since God is active each hour. What we do can improve (or worsen) our immediate situation. While we look for any quick victory over evil, yet we may still expect what Francis Schaeffer has called "substantial healing"—not a fundamental transformation of the overall human condition, but real changes that bring real fruits of justice and peace into our lives and into the lives of our neighbors. What we do does, by God's mercy, make a difference here and now and in the future. The apostle Peter even speaks of this as "waiting for and hastening the coming of the day of God" (2 Pet. 3:12).

Working in Hope

Many Christians, particularly fundamentalists and dispensationalists, spend a great deal of energy and ingenuity trying to determine the time of the Lord's return. In doing this they often give fantastic meanings to some Scripture passages, and ignore many elements of clear scriptural teaching.[2] As Calvinists we believe firmly that we must live in full expectation of our Lord's return, but without stargazing or by treating the Bible like a crystal ball. We must remember that Jesus himself said that "of that day and hour no one knows" (Matt. 24:36).

In preparing for the Lord's return we are not to spend our time trying to calculate the date or sitting around waiting for his appearance. Paul criticized members of the Thessalonian church for doing this (2 Thess. 3:6–13). They stopped working and idly waited for Jesus' return even after Paul had told them "as to the times and the seasons . . . you have no need to have anything written to you. For you yourselves know well that the day of the Lord will come like a thief in the night" (1 Thess. 5:1–2). Jesus' parables emphasize the same themes. Focusing on the end of the age, he told of the five wise and the five foolish virgins. The wise took oil for their lamps while the foolish did not. When the bridegroom suddenly appeared the foolish ones had no oil, nor the opportunity to buy any, and so they were shut out of the banquet (Matt. 25:1–12). Hence Jesus told his disciples, "Watch, therefore, for you know neither the day nor the hour" (Matt. 25:13).

The way for us to await the Lord's return is simply to be faithful in doing the things he has told us to do. The way to be ready is simply to be diligent about our Father's business. We are to preach the Word, to raise our children, to make a proper living, to be politically active, and to be responsible in every way until he comes. When he returns we know that our work will be accepted, not because we are perfect or have done such wonderful things, but because through Jesus Christ we are accepted as God's children. Our works are not judged according to the standard of the law but are accepted in God's grace.

> Those bound by the yoke of the law are like servants assigned certain tasks for each day by their masters. These servants think they have accomplished nothing, and dare not appear before their masters unless they have fulfilled the exact measure of their tasks. But sons, who are more generously and candidly treated by their fathers, do not hesitate to offer them incomplete

> and half-done and even defective works, trusting that their obedience and readiness of mind will be accepted by their fathers, even though they have not quite achieved what their fathers intended. Such children ought we to be, firmly trusting that our services will be approved by our most merciful Father, however small, rude, and imperfect these may be.[3]

Therefore we wait with hope and great joy. We need not fear the rejection of our imperfect works. Instead we believe that God will accept and perfect them. The world itself will be renewed at Christ's coming and there will be new heavens and a new earth. Together we may pray for that day when a loud voice will sound forth:

> Behold, the dwelling of God is with men. He will dwell with them, and they shall be his people, and God himself will be with them; he will wipe away every tear from their eyes, and death shall be no more, neither shall there be mourning nor crying nor pain any more, for the former things have passed away. (Rev. 21:3–4)

Then we will know even as we have been known. The veil of sin over our eyes will finally be removed and the Lord will be revealed in his majesty and sovereignty. We will see how he has ruled all of our lives, and all that has been, is, or will be. Like the elders before the throne we will sing:

> Worthy are thou, our Lord and God,
> to receive glory and honour and power,
> for thou didst create all things,
> and by thy will they existed and were created. (Rev. 4:11)

With every creature we will proclaim, "To him who sits upon the throne and to the Lamb be blessing and honor and glory and might for ever and ever" (Rev. 5:13).

Endnotes

Chapter 1

1. Georgia Harkness, *John Calvin: The Man and His Ethics* (New York: Henry Holt, 1931), p. 258.

2. For a survey of the literature on this subject, see W. Hastie, *The Theology of the Reformed Church in Its Fundamental Principles* (Edinburgh, 1904); H. Voigt, *Fundamental Dogmatik* (Gothal, 1874); H. Bauke, *Die Probleme der Theologie Calvins* (Giessen: Alfred Topelmann, 1910); H. H. Meeter, *The Fundamental Principle of Calvinism* (Grand Rapids: Eerdmans, 1930).

3. Hastie, *Theology of the Reformed Church,* p. 142.

4. Reinhold Seeberg, *Lehrbuch der Dogmengeschichte,* 2.2.558–59.

5. Wilhelm Dilthey, "Die Glaubenslehre der Reformation," in *Preuss. Jahrbuch* 1894, p. 80. Quoted in Bauke, *Probleme,* p. 25.

6. Meeter, *Fundamental Principle,* pp. 51–55.

7. Mason W. Pressly, "Calvinism and Science," in *Ev. Repertoire 1891,* p. 662.

8. B. B. Warfield, *Calvin as a Theologian and Calvinism Today* (Philadelphia: Presbyterian Board of Publication, 1909), pp. 23–24.

9. Ibid., pp. 22–23.

10. Charles Hodge, *Systematic Theology* (London: Thomas Nelson, 1872), 1: 548.

11. E. Doumergue, *Jean Calvin,* 4:357. Quoted in Bauke, *Probleme,* p. 84.

12. H. Bavinck, *Christelijke Wetenschap* (Kampen: J. H. Kok, 1913); Bavinck, *Gereformeerde Dogmatiek* (Kampen: J. H. Kok, 1911), 1: 237, 309–10; D. H. Th. Vollenhoven, *Het Calvinisme en de Reformatie van de Wijsbegeerte* (Amsterdam: H. J. Paris, 1933), pp. 20–21.

Chapter 3

1. H. Bavinck, *Gereformeerde Dogmatiek,* (Kampen: J. H. Kok, 1906), 1: 642.

2. Ibid., p. 634.

3. W. G. T. Shedd, *A History of Christian Doctrine,* 10th ed. (New York: Charles Scribner's Sons, 1881), 1:164. See also Caspar Wistar Hodge, Jr., "Finality of the Christian Religion," in *Biblical and Theological Studies* (New York: Charles Scribner's Sons, 1912), pp. 446–92.

Chapter 6

1. John Calvin, *Institutes of the Christian Religion,* trans. John Allen (Philadelphia: Presbyterian Board of Publication, 1921), 2.2.15. See also the context (2.2.13–17).

2. Ibid., 2.3.3.

3. Ibid.

4. Ibid.

5. Ibid., 2.16.4, quoting Augustine.

6. John Calvin, *Calvin's Calvinism: A Treatise on the Eternal Predestination of God* (London: Sovereign Grace Union, n.d.), pp. 26, 269–70.

Chapter 7

1. W. T. Herridge, article on culture in *Presbyterian Review,* 9:389.

2. John Calvin, *Institutes of the Christian Religion,* trans. John Allen (Philadelphia: Presbyterian Board of Publication, 1921), 4.2.15.

Chapter 8

1. A. M. Fairbairn, in *Cambridge Modern History* (New York: Macmillan, 1918), 2: 364. Used by permission.

2. Jean Jacques Rousseau, *Du Contrat Social,* 2.7 n. Quoted in Georgia Harkness, *John Calvin: The Man and His Ethics* (New York: Henry Holt, 1931), p. 221.

Chapter 9

1. John Calvin, *Institutes of the Christian Religion,* trans. John Allen (Philadelphia: Presbyterian Board of Publication, 1921), 4.20.2.

2. C. Smeenck, *Christelijk-Sociale Beginselen* (Kampen: J. H. Kok, 1934), pp. 36, 42, 50.

Chapter 10

1. P. A. Diepenhorst, *Ons Isolement* (Kampen: J. H. Kok, 1935), p. 33.

2. A. Kuyper, *Gemeene Gratie* (Amsterdam: Hoveker and Wormser, 1904), 3: 272–73.

3. H. Bavinck, *Gereformeerde Dogmatiek* (Kampen: J. H. Kok, 1906), 3: 547; A. Kuyper, *Gemeene Gratie,* 3:270, 277, 284–90. See also chap. 16.

Chapter 11

1. Woodrow Wilson, *The State: Elements of Historical and Practical Politics,* 2d ed. (Boston: D. C. Heath, 1898), p. 461.
2. Ibid., p. 469.
3. Ibid., pp. 506–7.

Chapter 12

1. Ernst Troeltsch, *The Social Teachings of the Christian Churches* (New York: Macmillan, 1931), 2: 903–4 n. 362, citing Choisy.
2. Ibid., p. 536.
3. Ibid., p. 621. Used by permission.

Chapter 13

1. Cf. Prov. 8:15; 1 Pet. 2:14.
2. John Calvin, *Institutes of the Christian Religion,* trans. John Allen (Philadelphia: Presbyterian Board of Publication, 1921), 4.20.25.
3. *Belgic Confession,* art. 36.

Chapter 14

1. John Calvin, *Institutes of the Christian Religion,* trans. John Allen (Philadelphia: Presbyterian Board of Publication, 1921), 4.20.31.
2. Ernst Troeltsch, *The Social Teachings of the Christian Churches* (New York: Macmillan, 1931), 2: 640. Used by permission.
3. Williston Walker, *John Calvin: The Organizer of Reformed Protestantism, 1509–1564* (New York: Knickerbocker/G. P. Putnam's Sons, 1906), pp. 403–8.
4. Quoted from N. S. McFetridge, *Calvinism in History* (Philadelphia: Presbyterian Board of Publication, 1912).

Chapter 16

1. See H. H. Kuyper, in *Toelichting op de Schetsen Kerkeschiedenis* (Vereeniging de Gereformeerde Jongelingsbond, 1936), 1: 338.
2. Philip Schaff, *The Creeds of Christendom* (New York: Harper, 1919), 1. 800.

Chapter 17

1. John Bassett Moore, "Recent History and Development of International Law," in *Encyclopedia Americana,* vol. 8 (New York: Americana, 1904).

Chapter 18

1. D. P. D. Fabius, *Volkenrecht* (Amsterdam: J. W. A. Van Schaik, 1907).
2. See Gen. 11; F. W. Grosheide, *National en Internationaal naar de Schrift* (Kampen: J. H. Kok, 1920).

Chapter 20

1. Charles Hodge, *Systematic Theology* (New York: Charles Scribner, 1873), 3: 365.

2. See, for example, the extensive lists of literature on peace movements in any modern encyclopedia.

Chapter 21

1. John Calvin, *Institutes of the Christian Religion,* trans. John Allen (Philadelphia: Presbyterian Board of Publication, 1921), 4.20.11.

Chapter 23

1. Herman Colyn, "Het Karakter der Anti-Revolutionaire Partij," in *Schrift en Historie* (Kampen: J. H. Kok, 1929), p. 26.

2. *Westminster Confession of Faith,* 23.11.

3. William Adams Brown, *Church and State in Contemporary America* (New York: Charles Scribner's Sons, 1936), p. 128 n. 42.

Chapter 24

1. Abraham Kuyper, *Christianity and the Class Struggle,* trans. D. Jellema (Grand Rapids: Piet Hein, 1950), p. 17.

2. Ibid., pp. 56–57.

3. Ibid., pp. 14 n. 1, 57.

4. John Calvin, *Institutes of the Christian Religion,* trans. John Allen (Philadelphia: Presbyterian Board of Publication, 1921), 4.20.4.

5. Kuyper, *Christianity and the Class Struggle,* p. 47.

6. Karl Marx, *Early Writing,* ed. T. Bottomore (New York: McGraw Hill, 1964), pp. 44, 155. See the comments of J. Miguez Bonino: "Nobody (whether Marxist or not) can become a Christian without repentance and conversion. Not a conversion from Marx to the church, but from sin to Jesus Christ" (*Christians and Marxists* [Grand Rapids: Eerdmans, 1976], p. 126).

7. Kuyper, *Christianity and the Class Struggle,* p. 2.

8. Ibid., p. 61.

9. Ibid., p. 57. Kuyper emphasized these same themes in his final speech, "What Now?" delivered on May 2, 1918, in Utrecht. See McKendree R. Langley, *The Practice of Political Spirituality* (Jordan Station: Paideia, 1984), p. 157.

Chapter 25

1. See Richard Mouw, *When the Kings Come Marching In* (Grand Rapids: Eerdmans, 1983).

2. See C. Vanderwaal, *Hal Lindsey and Biblical Prophecy* (Jordan Station: Paideia, 1978).

3. John Calvin, *Institutes of the Christian Religion,* trans. John Allen (Philadelphia: Presbyterian Board of Publication, 1921), 3.19.5.

Bibliography

Compiled by Peter De Klerk

Bibliographies

De Klerk, Peter. "Calvin Bibliographies, 1960– ," *Calvin Theological Journal* 7(1972): 221–50; 9(1974): 38–73, 210–40; 10(1975): 175–207; 11(1976): 199–243; 12(1977): 164–87; 13(1978): 166–94; 14(1979): 187–212; 15(1980): 244–60; 16(1981): 206–21; 17(1982): 231–47; 18(1983): 206–24; 19(1984): 192–212; 20(1985): 268–80; 21(1986): 194–221; 22(1987): 275–94; 23(1988): 195–221; 24(1989): 278–99.

De Koster, Lester Ronald. "Living Themes in the Thought of John Calvin: A Bibliographical Study." Ph.D. diss., University of Michigan, 1964.

Erichson, Alfred. *Bibliographia Calviniana.* Catalogus Chronologicus Operum Calvini. Catalogus Systematicus Operum quae sunt de Calvino cum indice Auctorum Alphabetico. Nieuwkoop: B. de Graaf, 1960.

Kempff, Dionysius. *A Bibliography of Calviniana, 1959–1974.* Studies in Medieval and Reformation Thought, 15. Leiden: E. J. Brill, 1975.

Niesel, Wilhelm. *Calvin-Bibliographie, 1901–1959.* München: Chr. Kaiser Verlag, 1961.

Tylenda, Joseph N. "Calvin Bibliography 1960–1970," edited by Peter De Klerk, *Calvin Theological Journal* 6(1971): 156–93.

Life and Teachings of John Calvin

Allen, Joseph Henry. *Three Phases of Modern Theology: Calvinism, Unitarianism, Liberalism.* Boston: George H. Ellis, 1880.

Alston, Wallace M., Jr. *The Church.* Guides to the Reformed Tradition. Atlanta: John Knox, 1984.

Armstrong, Brian Gary. *Calvinism and the Amyraut Heresy: Protestant Scholasticism and Humanism in Seventeenth Century France.* Madison: University of Wisconsin Press, 1969.

Audin, Jean Marie Vincent. *History of the Life, Works, and Doctrines of John Calvin.* Louisville: B. J. Webb & Brother, 1847.

Balke, Willem. *Calvin and the Anabaptist Radicals.* Grand Rapids: Eerdmans, 1981.

Beattie, Francis Robert. *Calvinism and Modern Thought.* Philadelphia: Westminster, 1901.

Beck, Frank B. *The Five Points of Calvinism.* Nundah: Covenanter, 1973.

Bell, M. Charles. *Calvin and Scottish Theology: The Doctrine of Assurance.* Edinburgh: Handsel, 1985.

Berk, Stephen E. *Calvinism versus Democracy: Timothy Dwight and the Origins of American Evangelical Orthodoxy.* Hamden: Archon, 1974.

Bèze, Théodore de. *The Life of John Calvin.* Philadelphia: J. Whetham, 1836.

Biéler, André. *The Social Humanism of Calvin.* Richmond: John Knox, 1964.

Blackburn, William Maxwell. *The College Days of Calvin.* Philadelphia: Presbyterian Board of Publication, 1865.

_____. *William Farel, and the Story of the Swiss Reform.* Philadelphia: Presbyterian Board of Publication, 1865.

_____. *Young Calvin in Paris, and the Little Flock That He Fed.* Philadelphia: Presbyterian Board of Publication and Sabbath School Work, 1865.

Boettner, Loraine. *The Reformed Doctrine of Predestination.* Grand Rapids: Eerdmans, 1932.

Bonar, Horatius. *The Five Points of Calvinism. In a Series of Letters by Horatius Bonar, Andrew Fuller, John Calvin, John Gill, Thomas Goodwin, and Jonathan Edwards.* Evanston: Sovereign Grace Book Club, 1957.

Bouwsma, William James. *John Calvin: A Sixteenth-Century Portrait.* New York: Oxford University Press, 1988.

Bratt, John Harold, ed. *The Rise and Development of Calvinism: A Concise History.* Grand Rapids: Eerdmans, 1959.

_____. *The Heritage of John Calvin.* Heritage Hall Lectures, 1960–70, Heritage Hall Publications, 2. Grand Rapids: Eerdmans, 1973.

Breen, Quirinus. *John Calvin: A Study in French Humanism.* Grand Rapids: Eerdmans, 1931.

Bungener, Laurence Louis Félix. *Calvin: His Life, His Labours, and His Writings.* Edinburgh: T. & T. Clark, 1863.

Cadier, Jean. *The Man God Mastered: A Brief Biography of John Calvin.* Grand Rapids: Eerdmans, 1960.

Clark, Francis. *Eucharistic Sacrifice and the Reformation.* Westminster: Newman; London: Darton, Longman & Todd, 1960.

Collins, Ross William. *Calvin and the Libertines of Geneva,* edited by F. D. Blackley. Toronto: Clarke, Irwin, 1968.

Conradie, A. L. *The Neo-calvinistic Concept of Philosophy: A Study in the Problem of Philosophic Communication.* Natal: University Press, 1960.

Crew, Phyllis Mack. *Calvinist Preaching and Iconoclasm in the Netherlands, 1544–1569.* London and New York: Cambridge University Press, 1978.

Dakin, Arthur. *Calvinism.* London: Duckworth, 1940.

d'Assonville, Victor Edouard. *John Knox and the Institutes of Calvin: A Few Points of Contact in Their Theology.* Durban: Drakensberg, 1968.

Davies, Alfred Mervyn. *Foundation of American Freedom.* Nashville: Abingdon, 1955.

Davies, Alfred T. *John Calvin and the Influence of Protestantism on National Life and Character.* London: Henry E. Walter, 1946.

_____. *John Calvin . . . Many-sided Genius.* New York: American Tract Society, 1947.

Davies, Rupert Eric. *The Problem of Authority in the Continental Reformers: A Study in Luther, Zwingli, and Calvin.* London: Epworth, 1946.

Douglass, Jane Dempsey. *Women, Freedom, and Calvin.* The 1983 Annie Kinkead Warfield Lectures. Philadelphia: Westminster, 1985.

Dowey, Edward Atkinson, Jr. *The Knowledge of God in Calvin's Theology.* New York: Columbia University Press, 1952.

Duffield, Gervase E., ed. *John Calvin.* Courtenay Studies in Reformation Theology, 1. Appleford: Abingdon/Sutton Courtenay, 1966.

Dyer, Thomas Henry. *The Life of John Calvin. Compiled from Authentic Sources, and Particularly from His Correspondence.* London: John Murray, 1850.

Eastaugh, Samuel. *Calvinism Not Founded on Truth.* Fakenham: E. E. Abbott, 1834.

Eby, Frederick. *Early Protestant Educators: The Educational Writings of Martin Luther, John Calvin, and Other Leaders of Protestant Thought.* New York: McGraw-Hill, 1931.

Eire, Carlos Mario Nieto. *War Against the Idols: The Reformation of Worship from Erasmus to Calvin.* Cambridge: Cambridge University Press, 1986.

Elliott-Binns, Leonard. *The Reformers and the Bible.* Cambridge: W. Heffer & Sons, 1923.

Ely, Ezra Stiles. *A Contrast Between Calvinism and Hopkinsianism.* New York: S. Whiting/Paul & Thomas, 1811.

Engel, Mary Potter. *John Calvin's Perspectival Anthropology.* American Academy of Religion, Academy Series, 52. Atlanta: Scholars, 1988.

Engelsma, David Jack. *Hyper-Calvinsim and the Call of the Gospel.* Grand Rapids: Reformed Free Publishing Association, 1980.

Faber, George Stanley. *Thoughts on the Calvinistic and Arminian Controversy.* London: F. C. and J. Rivington, 1804.

Farrington, Evelyn Maud. *Calvin, the Modern Man.* Belfast: Belfast Newsletter, 1953.

Feenstra, C. A. *Calvinism in the Light of God's Word (or God's Word versus Man's Words).* Sioux Center: Printed by the author, 1968.

Fisk, Wilbur. *Calvinistic Controversy. Embracing a Sermon on Predestination and Election, and Several Numbers on the Same Subject, Originally Published in the Christian Advocate and Journal.* New York: T. Mason and G. Lane, 1837.

Forstman, H. Jackson. *Word and Spirit: Calvin's Doctrine of Biblical Authority.* Stanford: Stanford University Press, 1962.

Foster, Randolph Sinks. *Objections to Calvinism as It Is, in a Series of Letters Addressed to Rev. N. L. Rice.* Cincinnati: Hitchcock & Walden, 1849.

Froude, James Anthony. *Calvinism.* An address delivered at St. Andrew's, March 17, 1871. New York: Charles Scribner, 1871.

Furcha, Edward J., ed. *In Honor of John Calvin, 1509–64.* Papers from the 1986 International Calvin Symposium, McGill University. ARC Supplement, 3. Montreal: Faculty of Religious Studies, McGill University, 1987.

Ganoczy, Alexandre. *The Young Calvin.* Philadelphia: Westminster, 1987.

Gerrish, Brian Albert. *The Old Protestantism and the New: Essays on the Reformation Heritage.* Chicago: University of Chicago Press, 1982.

Gerrish, Brian Albert, ed. *Reformatio Perennis: Essays on Calvin and the Reformation in Honor of Ford Lewis Battles.* Pittsburgh Theological Monograph Series, 32. Pittsburgh: Pickwick, 1981.

Girardeau, John Lafayette. *Calvinism and Evangelical Arminianism. Compared as to Election, Reprobation, Justification, and Related Doctrines.* Columbia: W. J. Duffie; New York: Baker & Taylor, 1890.

Glasgow, Frank T. *Calvin's Influence upon the political Development of the World.* Richmond: Whittet & Shepperson, n.d.

Good, Kenneth H. *Are Baptists Calvinists?* Oberlin: Regular Baptist Heritage Fellowship, 1975.

Graham, W. Fred. *The Constructive Revolutionary: John Calvin and His Socioeconomic Impact.* Richmond: John Knox, 1971.

Gray, Janet Glenn. *The French Huguenots: Anatomy of Courage.* Grand Rapids: Baker, 1981.

Green, Robert W., ed. *Protestantism and Capitalism: The Weber Thesis and Its Critics.* Problems in European Civilization. Boston: D. C. Heath, 1959.

Greaves, Richard L. *Theology and Revolution in the Scottish Reformation: Studies in the Thought of John Knox.* Grand Rapids: Christian University Press/Eerdmans, 1980.

Guizot, François Pierre Guillaume. *Great Christians of France: Saint Louis and Calvin.* London: Macmillan, 1878.

Hageman, Howard Garberich. *Pulpit and Table: Some Chapters in the History of Worship in the Reformed Churches.* Richmond: John Knox, 1962.

Hall, Basil. *John Calvin, Humanist and Theologian.* Historical Association Pamphlets, General Series, 33. London: Historical Association, 1967.

Hall, Charles A. M. *With the Spirit's Sword: The Drama of Spiritual Warfare in the Theology of John Calvin.* Basel Studies of Theology, 3. Richmond: John Knox, 1970.

Hancock, Ralph Cornel. *Calvin and the Foundations of Modern Politics.* Ithaca: Cornell University Press, 1987.

Hanko, Herman C., Homer Cooper Hoeksema, and Gise J. Van Baren. *The Five Points of Calvinism.* Mission Board of the Protestant Reformed Churches in America, 1967.

Harbison, Elmore Harris. *The Christian Scholar in the Age of the Reformation.* New York: Charles Scribner's Sons, 1956.

Hardwick, Charles. *A History of the Christian Church during the Reformation.* London: Macmillan, 1914.

Harkness, Georgia Elma. *John Calvin: The Man and His Ethics.* New York: Henry Holt, 1931.

Harris, D. Fisk. *Calvinism. Contrary to God's Word and Man's Moral Nature.* Harmar: Published by the author, 1890.

Harris, John Andrews. *The Calvinistic Doctrine of Election and Reprobation, No Part of St. Paul's Teachings.* Philadelphia: Porter & Coates, 1890.

Hastie, William. *The Theology of the Reformed Church in Its Fundamental Principles.* The Croall Lecture for 1892, edited by William Fulton. Edinburgh: T. & T. Clark, 1904.

Heller, Henry. *The Conquest of Poverty: The Calvinist Revolt in Sixteenth-Century France.* Studies in Medieval and Reformation Thought, 35. Leiden: E. J. Brill, 1986.

Helm, Paul. *Calvin and the Calvinists.* Edinburgh: Banner of Truth Trust, 1982.

Henderson, Henry F. *Calvin in His Letters.* London: J. M. Dent, 1909.

_____. *Religion in Scotland: Its Influence on National Life and Character.* The Chalmers Lectures, 1916–20. Paisley: Alexander Gardner, 1920.

Henry, Paul Emil. *The Life and Times of John Calvin, the Great Reformer.* 2 vols. New York: Robert Carter & Brothers, 1852–53.

Hepp, Valentine. *Calvinism and the Philosophy of Nature.* The Stone Lectures delivered at Princeton in 1930. Grand Rapids: Eerdmans, 1930.

Hesselink, Ira John, Jr. *On Being Reformed: Distinctive Characteristics and Common Misunderstandings.* Ann Arbor: Servant Books, 1983.

Higman, Francis Montgomery. *The Style of John Calvin in His French Polemical Treatises.* London: Oxford University Press, 1967.

Holl, Karl. *The Cultural Significance of the Reformation.* Cleveland: World, 1966.

Holwerda, David Eugene, ed. *Exploring the Heritage of John Calvin: Essays in Honor of John Harold Bratt.* Grand Rapids: Baker, 1976.

Hoogland, Marvin P. *Calvin's Perspective on the Exaltation of Christ in Comparison with the Post-Reformation Doctrine of the two States.* Kampen: J. H. Kok, 1966.

Hoogstra, Jacob Tunis, ed. *American Calvinism: A Survey.* Grand Rapids: Baker, 1957.

_____. *John Calvin, Contemporary Prophet: A Symposium.* Grand Rapids: Baker, 1959.

Höpfl, Harro. *The Christian Polity of John Calvin.* Cambridge Studies in the History and Theory of Politics. New York: Cambridge University Press, 1982.

Huizinga, Arnold van Couthen Piccardt. *The Calvinist View of State.* Breda: Drukkerij en Uitgeversmaatschappij v/h Broese & Peereboom, 1933.

Hunt, George Laird, ed. *Calvinism and the Political Order.* Essays prepared for the Woodrow Wilson Lectureship of the National Presbyterian Center, Washington, D.C. Philadelphia: Westminster, 1965.

Hunt, Robert Nigel Garew. *Calvin.* London: Centenary, 1933.

Hunter, Adam Mitchell. *The Teaching of Calvin: A Modern Interpretation.* Glasgow: Maclehose, Jackson, 1920.

Hyma, Albert. *Christianity, Capitalism and Communism: A Historical Analysis.* Ann Arbor: George Wahr, 1937.

_____. *The Life of John Calvin.* Grand Rapids: Eerdmans, 1943.

_____. *Renaissance to Reformation.* Grand Rapids: Eerdmans, 1951.

Innes, William C. *Social Concern in Calvin's Geneva.* Pittsburgh Theological Monograph, n.s., 7, edited by Susan Cembalisty-Innes. Allison Park: Pickwick, 1983.

Irwin, Clarke Huston. *John Calvin, the Man and His Work.* London: Religious Tract Society, 1909.

Jansen, John Frederick. *Calvin's Doctrine of the Work of Christ.* London: James Clark, 1956.

Johnson, Thomas Cary. *John Calvin and the Genevan Reformation: A Sketch.* Richmond: Presbyterian Committee of Publication, 1900.

Kendall, Robert Tillman. *Calvin and English Calvinism to 1649.* Oxford Theological Monographs. Oxford: Oxford University Press, 1979.

Kingdon, Robert McCune. *Geneva and the Coming of the Wars of Religion in France, 1555–1563.* Travaux d'Humanisme et Renaissance, 22. Genève: Librarie E. Droz, 1956.

_____. *Geneva and the Consolidation of the French Protestant Movement, 1564–1572: A Contribution to the History of Congregationalism, Presbyterianism, and Calvinist Resistance Theory.* Madison: University of Wisconsin Press, 1967.

Kingdon, Robert McCune, and Robert Dean Linder, eds. *Calvin and Calvinism: Sources of Democracy?* Problems in European Civilization. Lexington: D. C. Heath, 1970.

Kistemaker, Simon. *Calvinism: History, Principles, Perspectives.* Grand Rapids: Baker, 1966.

Klooster, Fred H. *Calvin's Doctrine of Predestination.* Baker Biblical Monograph. Grand Rapids: Baker, 1977.

Kromminga, Carl Gerhard. *Man before God's Face in Calvin's Preaching.* Calvin Theological Seminary Monograph Series, 2. Grand Rapids: Calvin Theological Seminary, 1961.

Kruithof, Bastian. *The High Points of Calvinism.* Grand Rapids: Baker, 1949.

Kuiper, Herman. *Calvin on Common Grace.* Goes: Oosterbaan & le Cointre; Grand Rapids: Smitter, 1928.

Kuyper, Abraham. *Calvinism: Six Stone Lectures.* Grand Rapids: Eerdmans, 1931.

Lane, George Eric. *What Is This Calvinism?* Red Hill: Sovereign Grace Union, 1968.

Lecerf, Auguste. *An Introduction to Reformed Dogmatics.* Lutterworth Library, 28. London: Lutterworth, 1949.

Lee, Francis Nigel. *Calvin on the Sciences.* London: Sovereign Grace Union, 1969.

Leith, John Haddon. *An Introduction to the Reformed Tradition: A Way of Being the Christian Community.* Atlanta: John Knox, 1977.

_____. *John Calvin's Doctrine of the Christian Life.* Louisville: Westminster/John Knox, 1989.

Lingle, Walter Lee, and John W. Kuykendall. *Presbyterians, Their History and Beliefs.* Atlanta: John Knox, 1978.

Louvet, Simone Lévêque. *Calvin: A Modern Biography,* by Jean Moura [pseud.] and Paul Louvet. Garden City: Doubleday, Doran, 1932.

McCrie, Thomas. *The Early Years of John Calvin: A Fragment, 1509–1536.* edited by William Ferguson. Edinburgh: David Douglas, 1880.

McDonnell, Kilian. *John Calvin, the Church, and the Eucharist.* Princeton: Princeton University Press, 1967.

McFetridge, Nathaniel S. *Calvinism in History.* Westminster Paper Series. Philadelphia: Presbyterian Board of Publication and Sabbath School Work, 1882.

McKee, Elsie Anne. *John Calvin on the Diaconate and Liturgical Almsgiving.* Genève: Librairie Droz, 1984.

Mackenzie, John. *Memoirs of the Life and Writings of John Calvin.* Compiled from the narrative of Theodore Beza, and other authentic documents, accompanied with biographical sketches of the Reformation. London: Williams & Smith, 1809.

Mackinnon, James. *Calvin and the Reformation.* London: Longmans, Green, 1936.

McNeill, John Thomas. *The History and Character of Calvinism.* New York: Oxford University Press, 1954.

Marshall, Gordon. *Presbyteries and Profits: Calvinism and the Development of Capitalism in Scotland, 1560–1707.* Oxford: Clarendon; New York: Oxford University Press, 1980.

Masselink, William. *Common Grace and Christian Education: A Calvinistic Philosophy of Science.* Chicago: Published by the author, 1951.

Miles, Robert Whitfield. *That Frenchman, John Calvin.* New York: Fleming H. Revell, 1939.

Milner, Benjamin Charles, Jr. *Calvin's Doctrine of the Church.* Studies in the History of Christian Thought, 5. Leiden: E. J. Brill, 1970.

Monsma, John Clover. *What Calvinism Has Done for America.* Chicago: Rand McNally, 1919.

Monter, E. William. *Studies in Genevan Government (1536–1605).* Travaux d'Humanisme et Renaissance, 62. Genève: Librairie Droz, 1964.

_____. *Calvin's Geneva.* New Dimensions in History: Historical Cities. New York: John Wiley & Sons, 1967.

Mueller, William A. *Church and State in Luther and Calvin: A Comparative Study.* Garden City: Doubleday, 1965.

Muller, Richard Alfred. *Christ and the Decree: Christology and Predestination in Reformed Theology from Calvin to Perkins.* Studies in Historical Theology, 2. Durham: Labyrinth, 1986.

Murray, John. *Calvin on Scripture and Divine Sovereignty.* Grand Rapids: Baker, 1960.

Niesel, Wilhelm. *The Theology of Calvin.* Philadelphia: Westminster, 1956.

Nixon, Leroy. *John Calvin, Expository Preacher.* Grand Rapids: Eerdmans, 1950.

_____. *John Calvin's Teachings on Human Reason: A Synthesis from Calvin's Writings According to Established Categories . . . and a Study of Their Implications for the Theory of Reformed Protestant Christian Education.* An Exposition-Testament Book. New York: Exposition, 1963.

Old, Hughes Oliphant, Jr. *The Patristic Roots of Reformed Worship.* Zürcher Beiträge zur Reformationsgeschichte, 5. Zürich: Theologischer Verlag, 1975.

Olson, Jeannine E. *Calvin and Social Welfare: Deacons and the Bourse Française.* Selinsgrove: Susquehanna University Press; London: Associated University Presses, 1988.

Osterhaven, Maurice Eugene. *The Spirit of the Reformed Tradition.* Grand Rapids: Eerdmans, 1971.

Palm, Franklin Charles. *Calvinism and the Religious Wars.* The Beckshire Studies in European History. New York: Henry Holt, 1932.

Parker, Thomas Henry Louis. *The Oracles of God: An Introduction to the Preaching of John Calvin.* London: Lutterworth, 1947.

_____. *The Doctrine of the Knowledge of God: A Study in the Theology of John Calvin.* Edinburgh: Oliver & Boyd, 1952.

_____. *Portrait of Calvin.* London: S.C.M., 1954.

_____. *Calvin's New Testament Commentaries.* Grand Rapids: Eerdmans, 1971.

_____. *John Calvin: A Biography.* London: J. M. Dent & Sons, 1975.

_____. *Calvin's Old Testament Commentaries.* Edinburgh: T. & T. Clark, 1986.

Partee, Charles Brooks. *Calvin and Classical Philosophy.* Studies in the History of Christian Thought, 14. Leiden: E. J. Brill, 1977.

Poggi, Gianfranco. *Calvinism and the Capitalist Spirit: Max Weber's Protestant Ethic.* Amherst: University of Massachusetts Press, 1983.

Potter, George Richard, and M. Greengrass. *John Calvin*. Documents of Modern History. New York: St. Martin's, 1983.

Prestwich, Menna, ed. *International Calvinism, 1541–1715*. Oxford: Clarendon; New York: Oxford University Press, 1985.

Quistorp, Heinrich. *Calvin's Doctrine of the Last Things*. London: Lutterworth, 1955.

Reed, Richard Clark. *The Gospel as Taught by Calvin*. Jackson: Presbyterian Reformation Society, n.d.

Reid, William Stanford, ed. *John Calvin: His Influence in the Western World*. Grand Rapids: Zondervan, 1982.

Reyburn, Hugh Young. *John Calvin: His Life, Letters, and Work*. London: Hodder & Stoughton, 1914.

Richard, Lucien Joseph. *The Spirituality of John Calvin*. Atlanta: John Knox, 1974.

Sanford, Elias B. *A History of the Reformation*. Hartford: S. S. Scranton, 1917.

Schmidt, Albert Marie. *John Calvin and the Calvinistic Tradition*. Men of Wisdom, 10. New York: Harper & Brothers; London: Longmans, 1960.

Schnucker, Robert Victor, ed. *Calviniana: Ideas and Influence of Jean Calvin*. Sixteenth Century Essays and Studies, 10. Kirksville: Sixteenth Century Journal, 1988.

Schulze, Ludolf Ferdinand. *Calvin's Reply to Pighius*. Human Sciences Research Council Publication Series, 9. Potchefstroom: Pro Rege, 1971.

_____. *Calvin and "Social Ethics": His Views on Property, Interest and Usury*. Pretoria: Kital, 1985.

Scott, John. *Calvin and the Swiss Reformation*. London: R. B. Seeley and W. Burnside, 1833.

Selinger, Suzanne. *Calvin Against Himself*. An Inquiry in Intellectual History. Hamden: Archon, 1984.

Sell, Alan P. F. *The Great Debate: Calvinism, Arminianism and Salvation*. Studies in Christian Thought and History. West Sussex: H. E. Walter, 1982.

Shedd, William Greenough Thayer. *Calvinism: Pure and Mixed. A Defence of the Westminster Standards*. New York: Charles Scribner's Sons, 1893.

Shepherd, Victor A. *The Nature and Function of Faith in the Theology of John Calvin*. National Association of Baptist Professors of Religion Dissertation Series, 2. Macon: Mercer University Press, 1983.

Singer, Charles Cregg. *John Calvin: His Roots and Fruits*. International Library of Philosophy and Theology Philosophical and Historical Studies Series. Philadelphia: Presbyterian & Reformed, 1967.

Smith, Egbert Watson. *The Creed of Presbyterians*. Richmond: John Knox, 1960.

Smith, Gary Scott. *The Seeds of Secularization: Calvinism, Culture, and Pluralism in America, 1870–1915*. Grand Rapids: Christian University Press/Eerdmans, 1985.

Smith, William Kyle. *Calvin's Ethics of War: A Documentary Study*. Annapolis: Published for the Westminster Foundation of Annapolis by Academic Fellowship, 1972.

Smyth, Thomas. *Calvin and His Enemies: A Memoir of the Life, Character, and Principles of John Calvin.* Philadelphia: Presbyterian Board of Publication, 1856.

Spier, J. M. *Christianity and Existentialism.* Philadelphia: Presbyterian & Reformed, 1953.

Stauffer, Richard André. *The Humanness of John Calvin.* Nashville: Abingdon, 1971.

Steele, David N., and Curtis C. Thomas. *The Five Points of Calvinism.* International Library of Philosophy and Theology Biblical and Theological Studies. Grand Rapids: Baker, 1963.

Stepanek, Sally. *John Calvin.* World Leaders, Past & Present. New York: Chelsea House, 1987.

Stevenson, Richard Taylor. *John Calvin: The Statesman.* Men of the Kingdom. New York: Abingdon, 1907.

Stickelberger, Emanuel. *Calvin.* London: James Clarke, 1959.

Strong, J. Selden. *The Essential Calvinism.* Boston: Pilgrim, 1909.

Stuermann, Walter Earl. *A Critical Study of Calvin's Concept of Faith.* Tulsa: Published for the author, 1952.

Tonkin, John. *The Church and the Secular Order in Reformation Thought.* New York: Columbia University Press, 1971.

Toon, Peter. *Puritans and Calvinism.* Swengel: Reiner, 1973.

Torrance, Thomas Forsyth. *Calvin's Doctrine of Man.* London: Lutterworth, 1949.

_____. *Kingdom and Church: A Study in the Theology of the Reformation.* Edinburgh: Oliver & Boyd, 1956.

Van Buren, Paul. *Christ in Our Place: The Substitutionary Character of Calvin's Doctrine of Reconciliation.* Edinburgh: Oliver & Boyd, 1957.

van der Walt, Barend Johannes, ed. *John Calvin's* Institutes: *His* Magnum Opus. Proceedings of the Second South African Congress for Calvin Research, July 31–August 3, 1984. Potchefstroom: Potchefstroom University for Higher Christian Education, 1986.

Van Til, Cornelius. *The Case for Calvinism.* International Library of Philosophy and Theology Philosophical and Historical Studies Series. Grand Rapids: Baker, 1964.

Van Til, Henry R. *The Calvinistic Concept of Culture.* Grand Rapids: Baker, 1959.

Vasady, Bela. *The Main Traits of Calvin's Theology.* Grand Rapids: Eerdmans, 1951.

Vollmer, Phillip. *John Calvin: Theologian, Preacher, Educator, Statesman.* Presented to the Reformed Churches holding the Presbyterian System, on the 400th Anniversary of the Reformer's Birth. With Contributions from J. I. Good and Wm. B. Roberts. Philadelphia: Presbyterian Board of Publication, 1909.

Vos, Arvin Paul. *Aquinas, Calvin, and Contemporary Protestant Thought: A Critique of Protestant Views on the Thought of Thomas Aquinas.* Washington: Christian University Press; Grand Rapids: Eerdmans, 1985.

Walker, Williston. *John Calvin: The Organiser of Reformed Protestantism, 1509–1564*. Heroes of the Reformation. New York: G. P. Putnam's Sons, 1906.

Wallace, Ronald Stewart. *Calvin's Doctrine of the Word and Sacrament*. Edinburgh: Oliver & Boyd, 1953.

_____. *Calvin's Doctrine of the Christian Life*. Edinburgh: Oliver & Boyd, 1959.

Walzer, Michael. *The Revolution of the Saints: A Study in the Origins of Radical Politics*. Cambridge: Harvard University Press, 1965.

Warburton, Ben A. *Calvinism: Historically and Doctrinally Considered*. London: C. J. Farncombe & Sons, 1913.

Warfield, Benjamin Breckinridge. *Calvin and Calvinism*. New York: Oxford University Press, 1931.

_____. *Calvin and Augustine*, edited by Samuel G. Craig. Philadelphia: Presbyterian & Reformed, 1956.

Waterman, Elijah. *Memoirs of the Life and Writings of John Calvin*. Together with a selection of letters written by him, and other distinguished Reformers: also, notes, and biographical sketches of some of his contemporaries. Boston: Cummings & Hilliard, 1813.

Weber, Max. *The Protestant Ethic and the Spirit of Capitalism*. New York: Charles Scribner's Sons, 1958.

Wendel, François. *Calvin: The Origins and Development of His Religious Thought*. New York: Harper & Row, 1963.

Whitney, Harold. *Profile of John Calvin and the Institutes*. Brisbane: W. R. Smith & Paterson, 1957.

Wileman, William. *John Calvin: His Life, His Teaching, and His Influence*. London: Robert Banks & Sons, 1909.

Willis, Edward David. *Calvin's Catholic Christology: The Function of the So-called "Extra Calvinisticum" in Calvin's Theology*. Studies in Medieval and Reformation Thought, 2. Leiden: E. J. Brill, 1966.

Wilterdink, Garret A. *Tyrant or Father? A Study of Calvin's Doctrine of God*. Scholastic Monograph Series. 2 vols. Bristol: Wyndham Hall, 1985.

Young, William. *Toward a Reformed Philosophy: The Development of a Protestant Philosophy in Dutch Calvinistic Thought since the Time of Abraham Kuyper*. Grand Rapids: Piet Hein; Franeker: T. Wever, 1952.

Index